XU YONG   **NEGATIVES**

These photographic negatives were taken 26 years ago, in 1989.

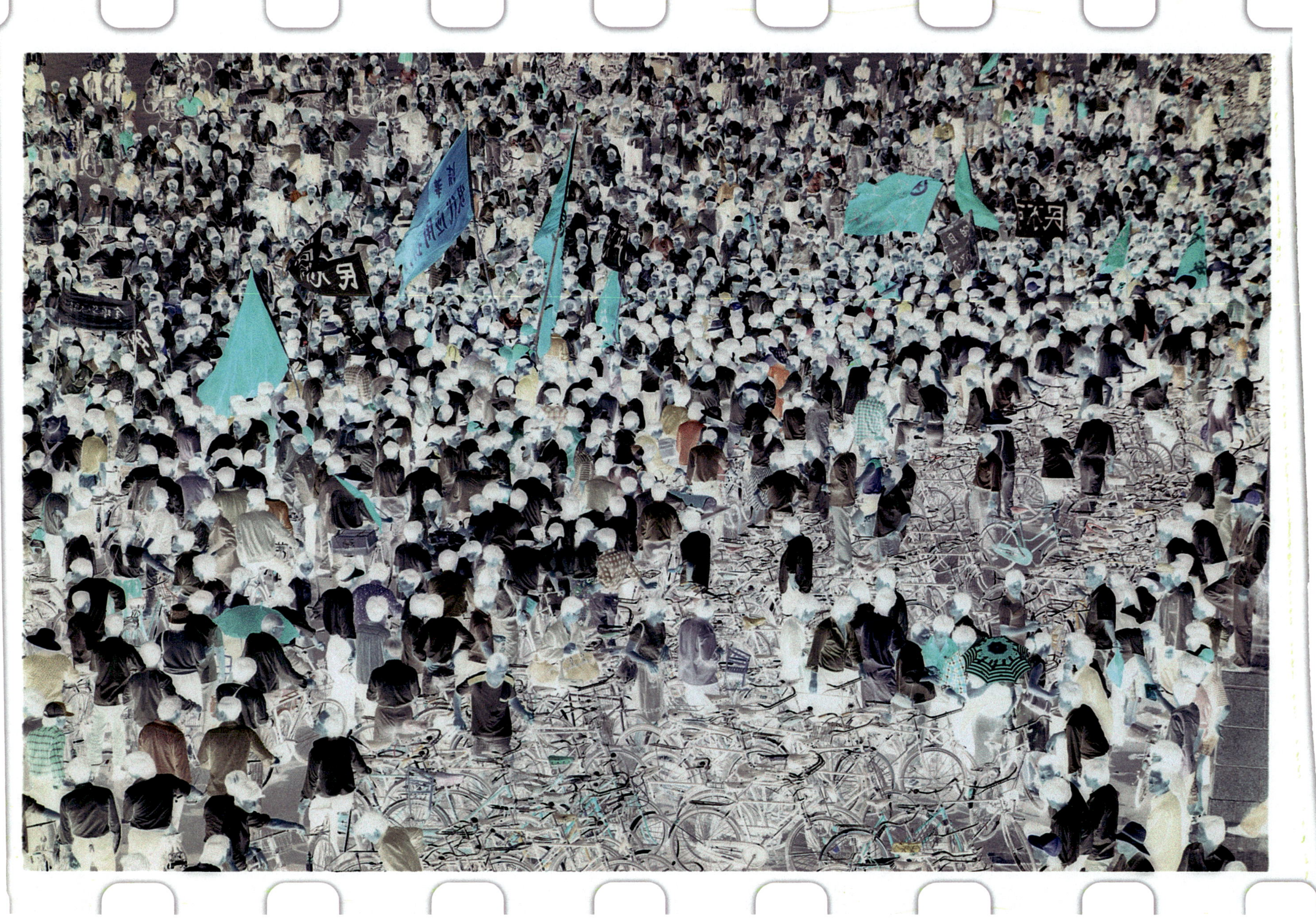

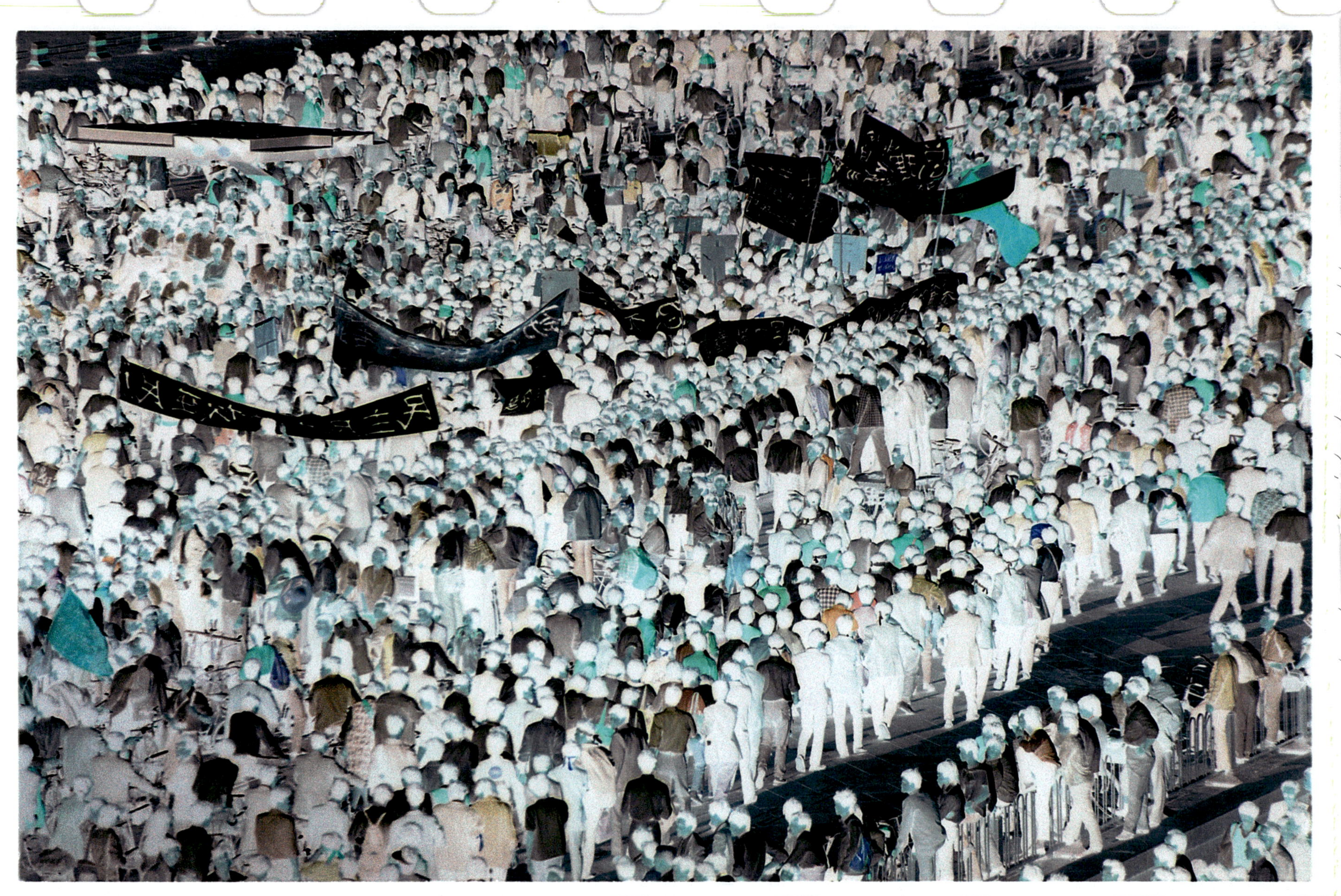

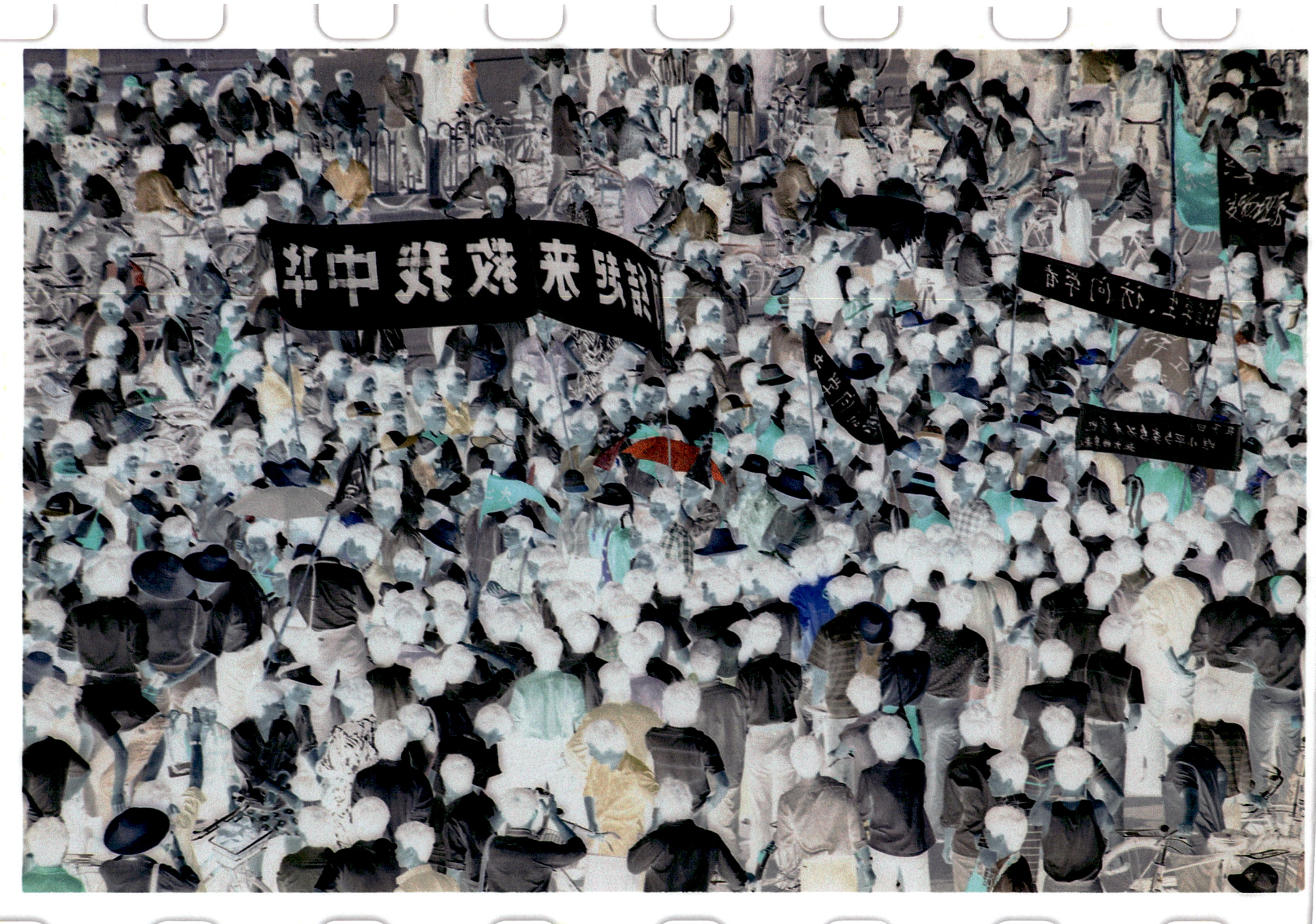

04

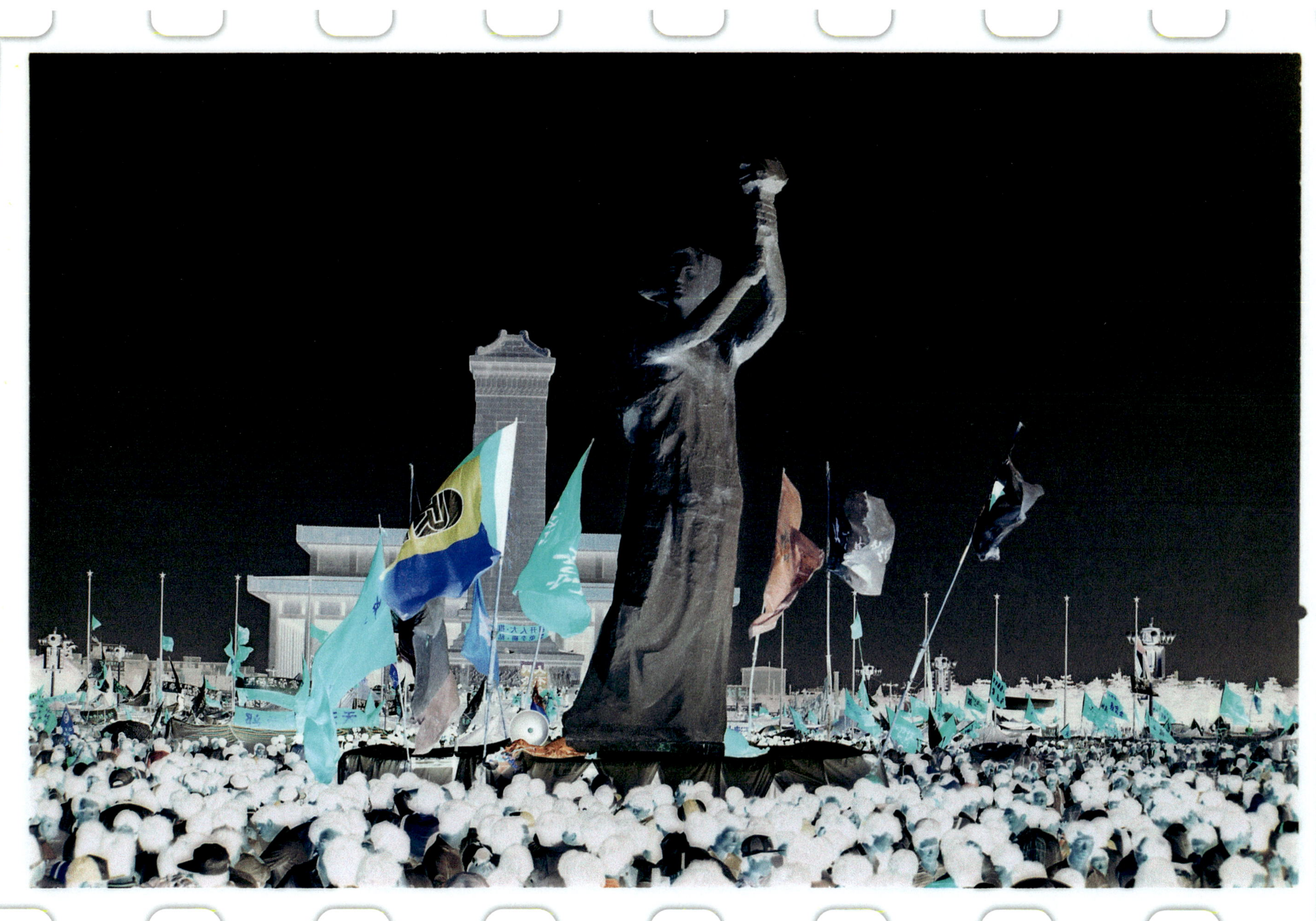

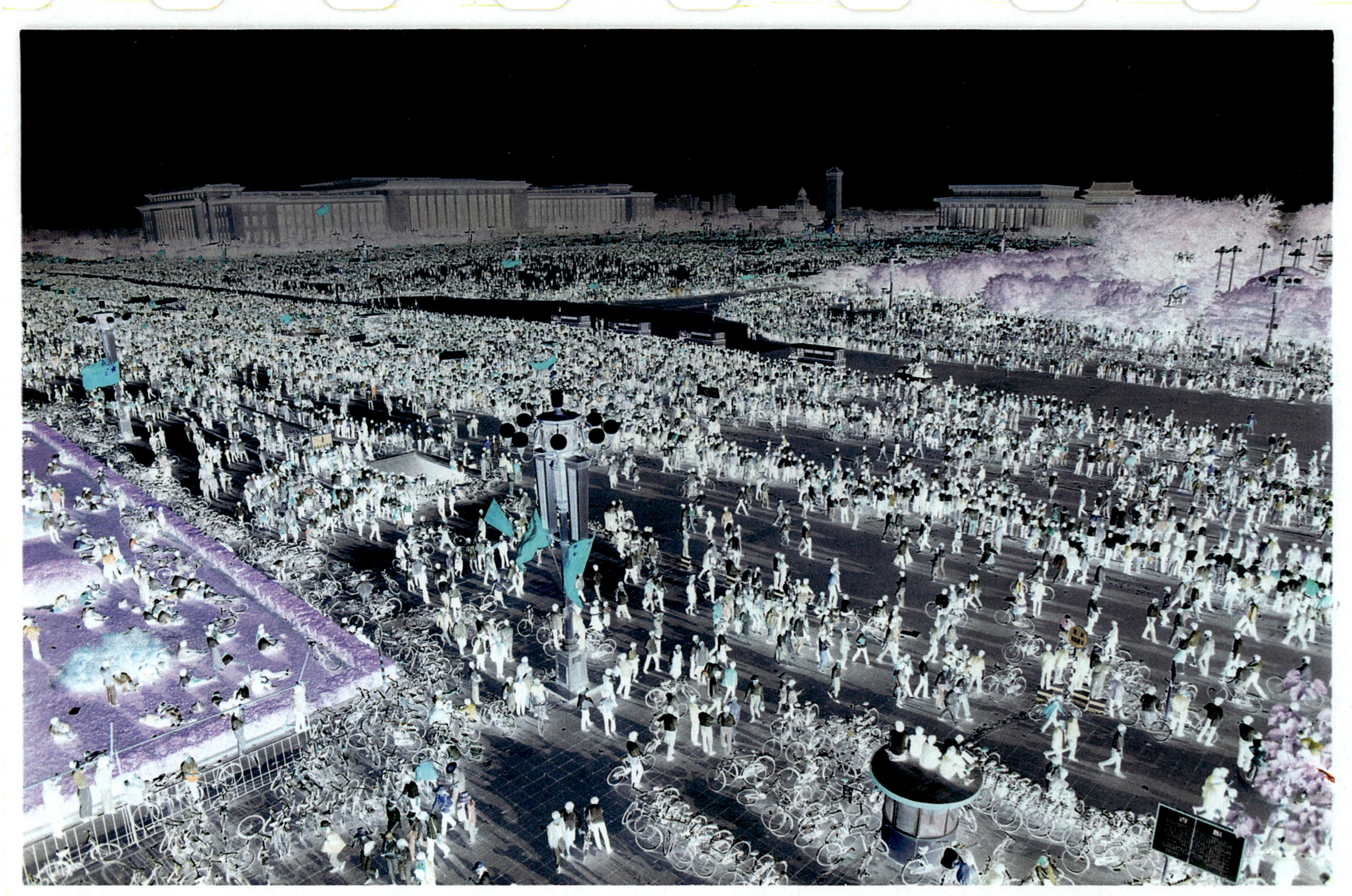

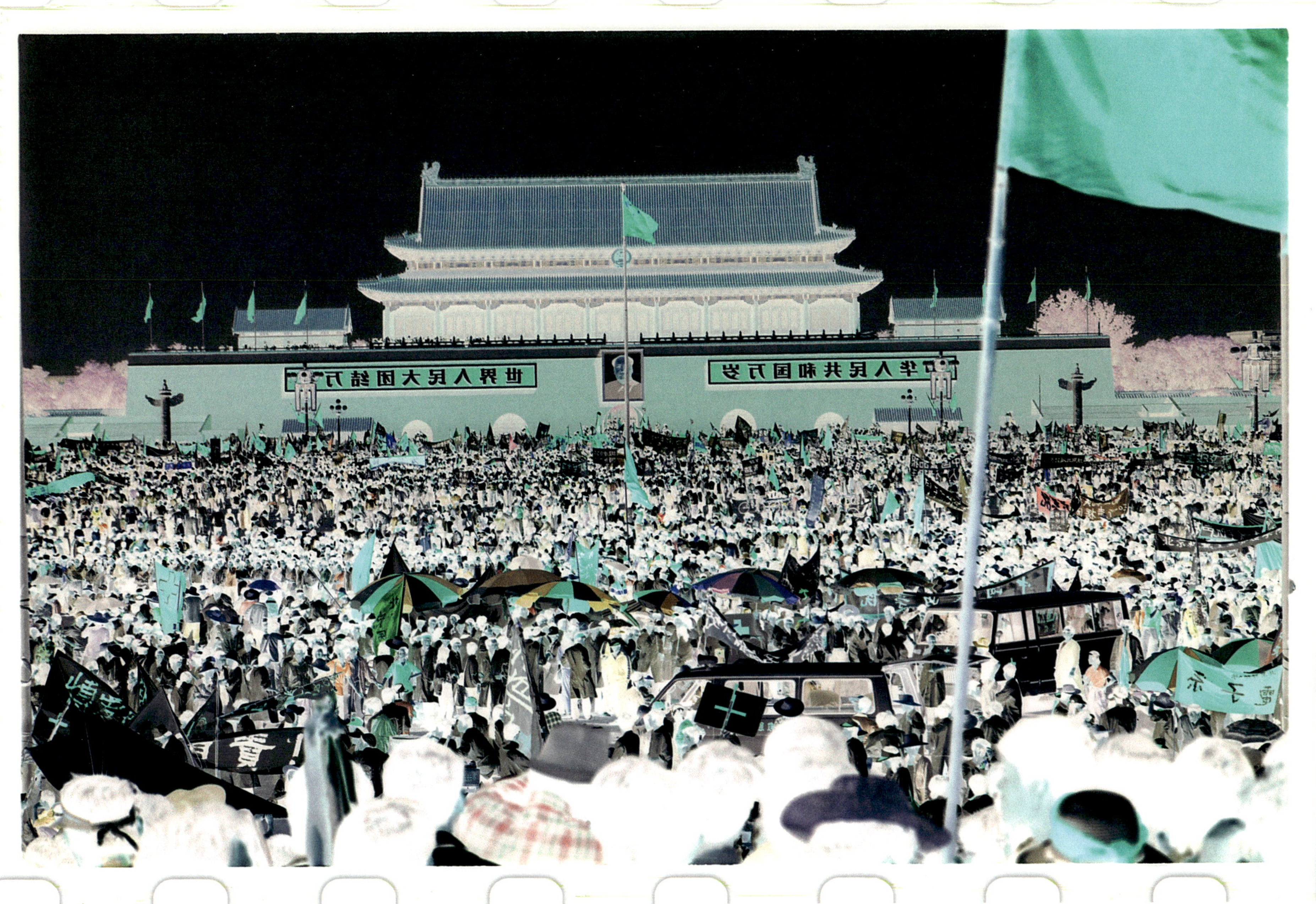

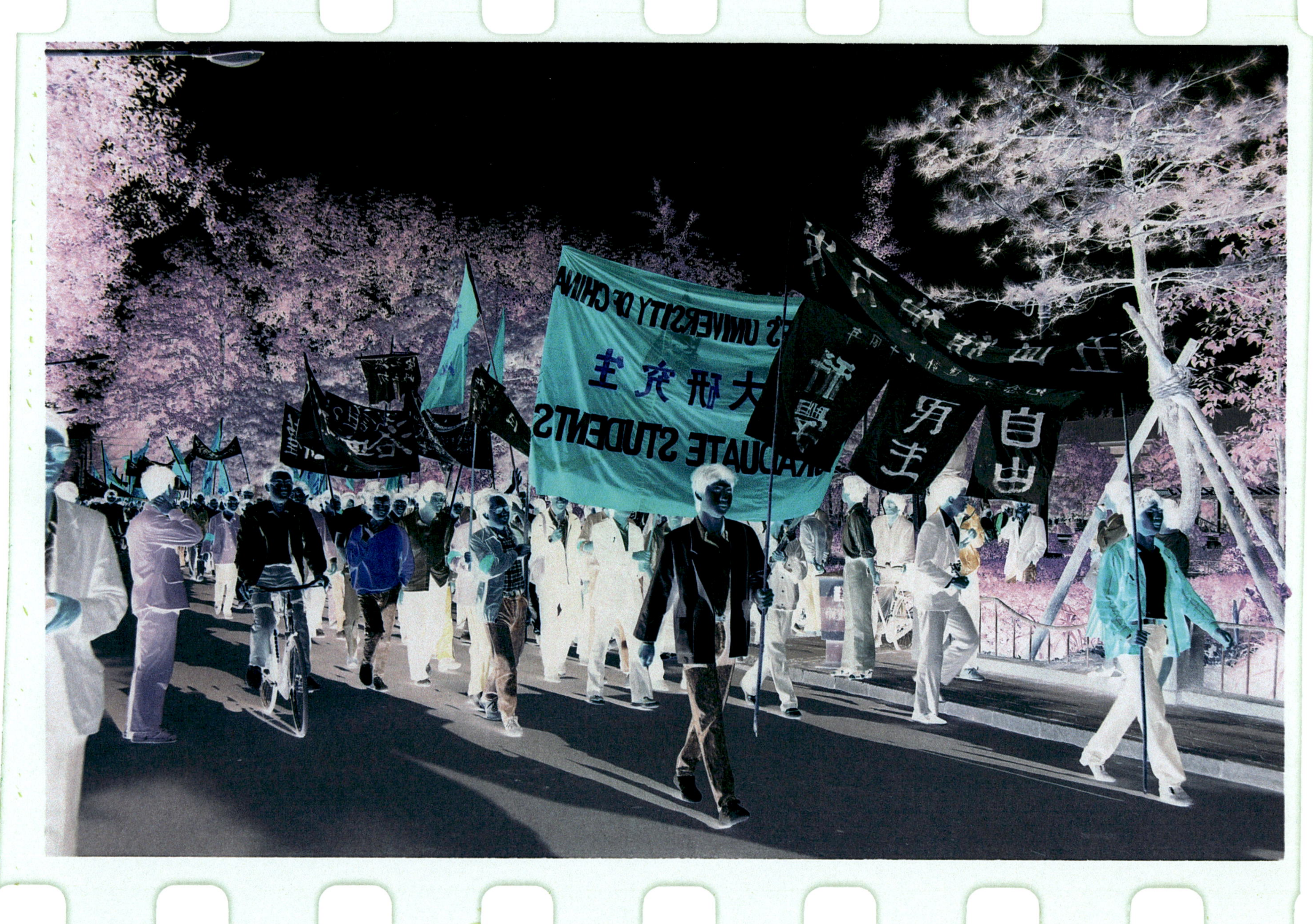

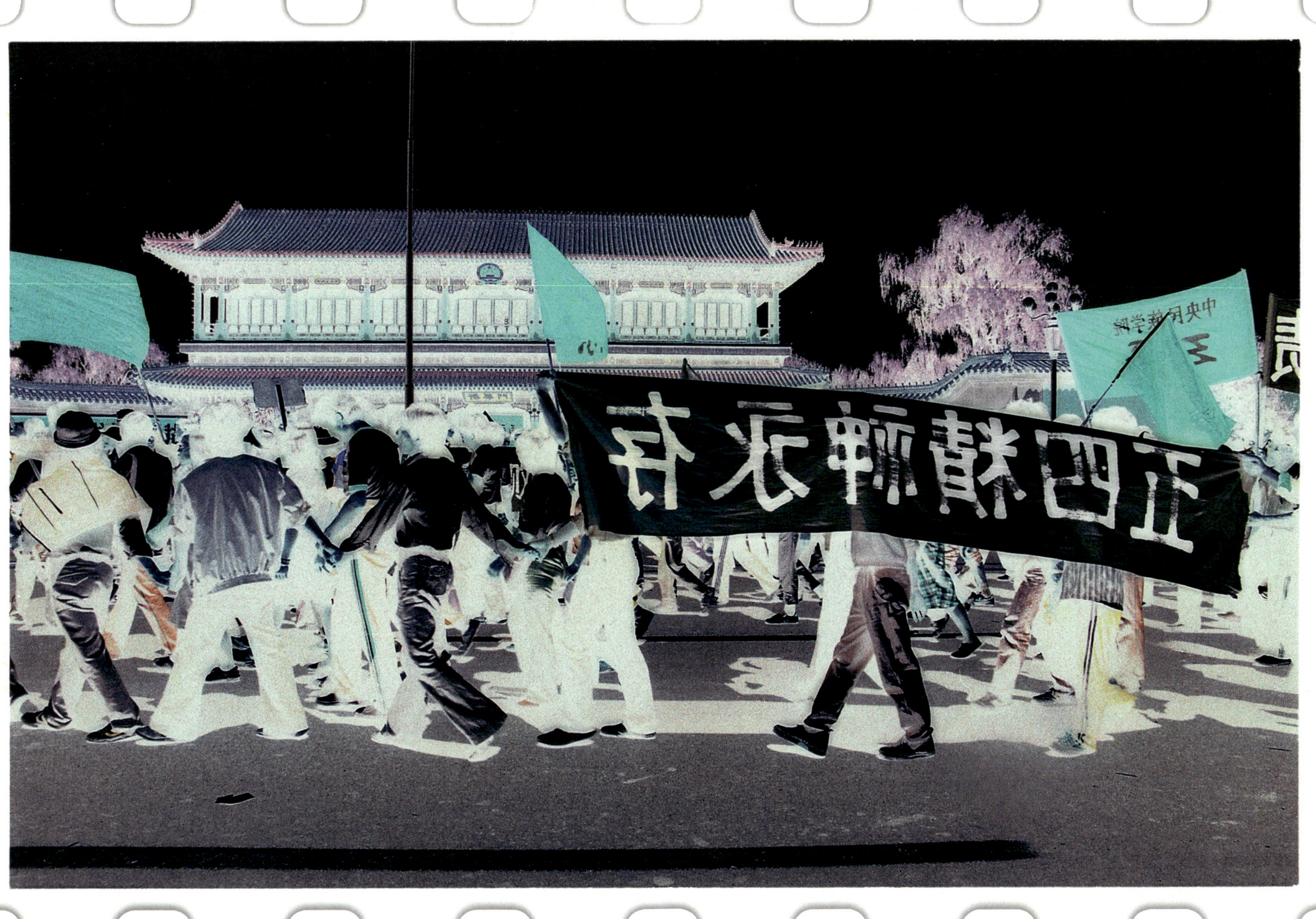

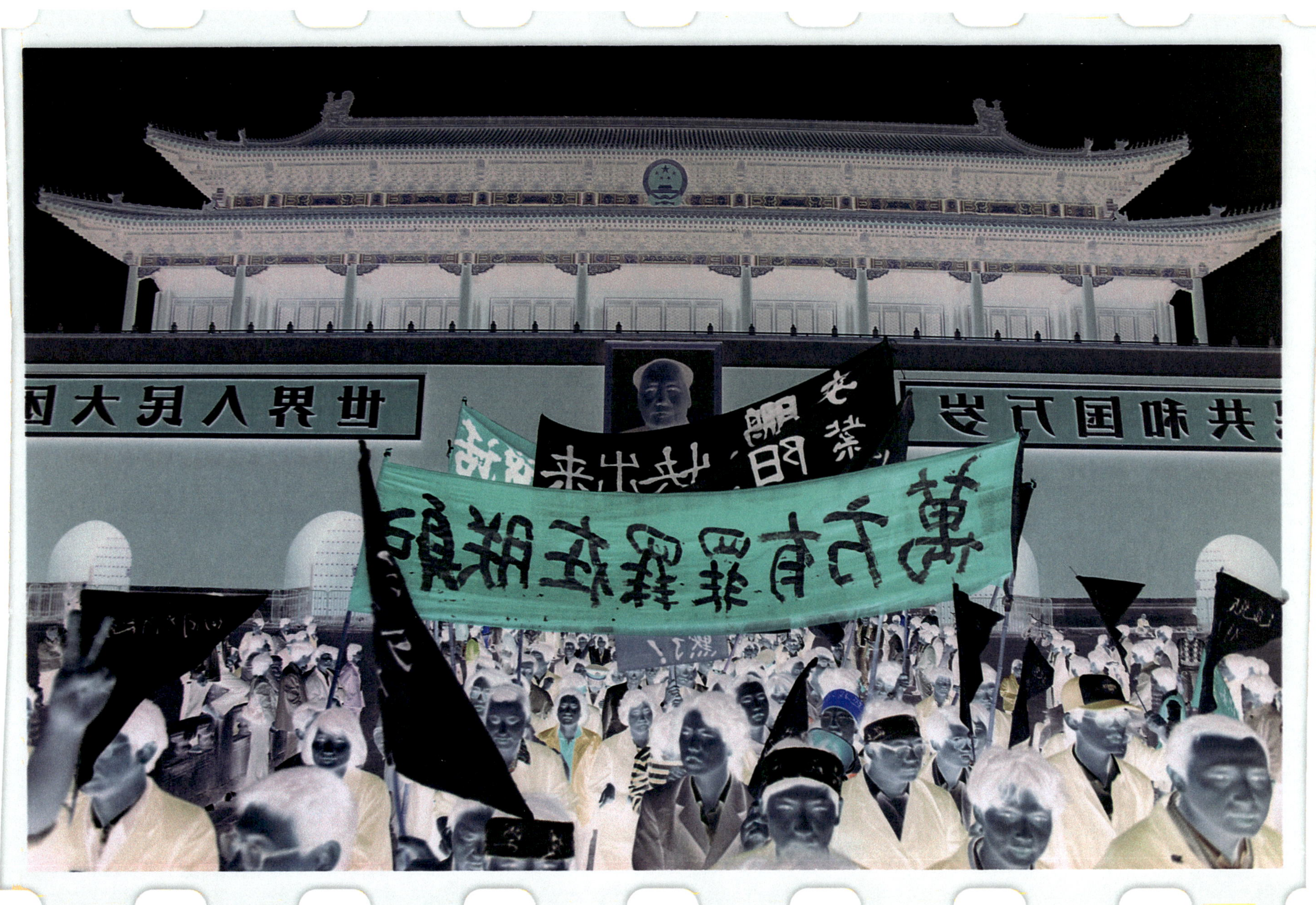

10

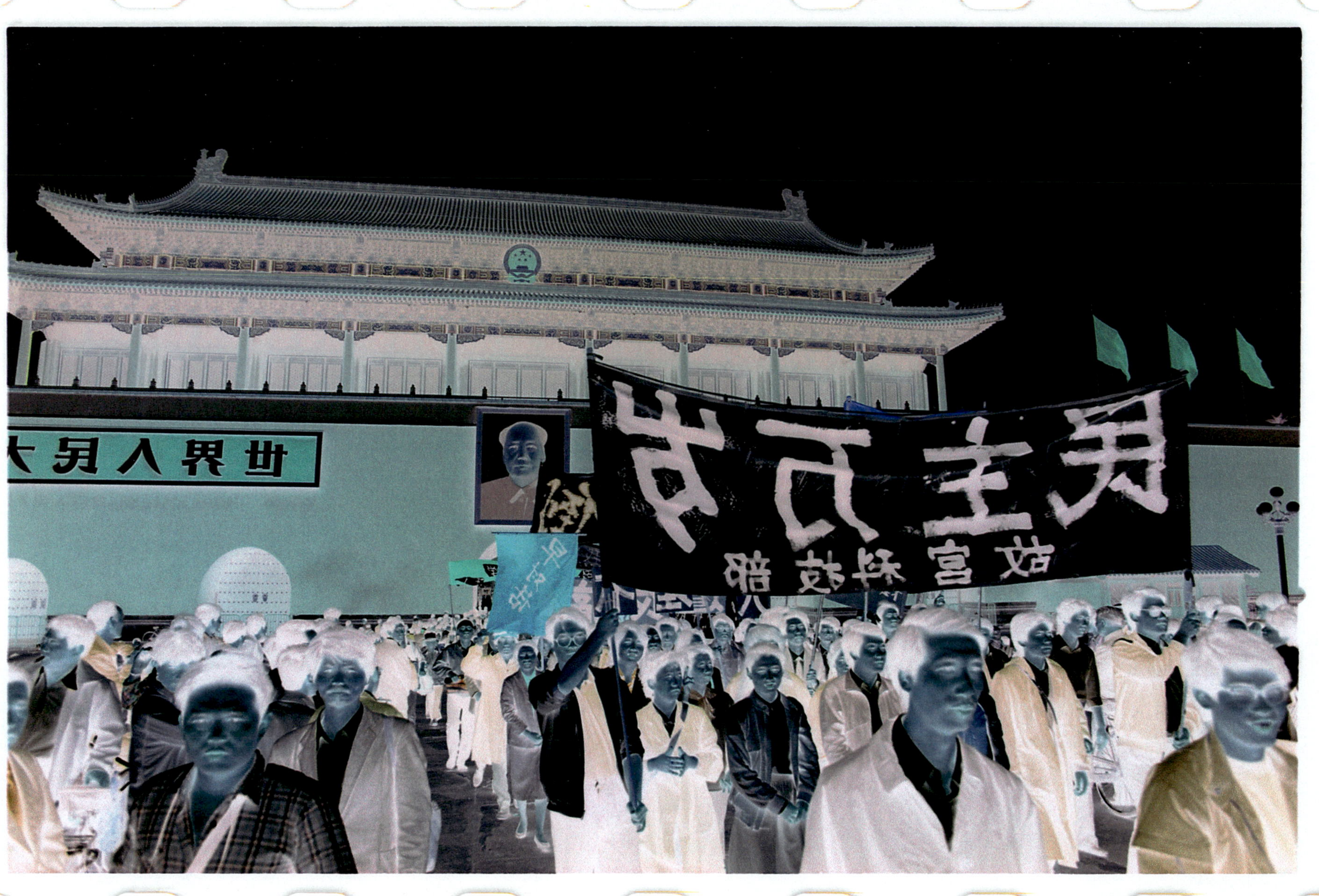

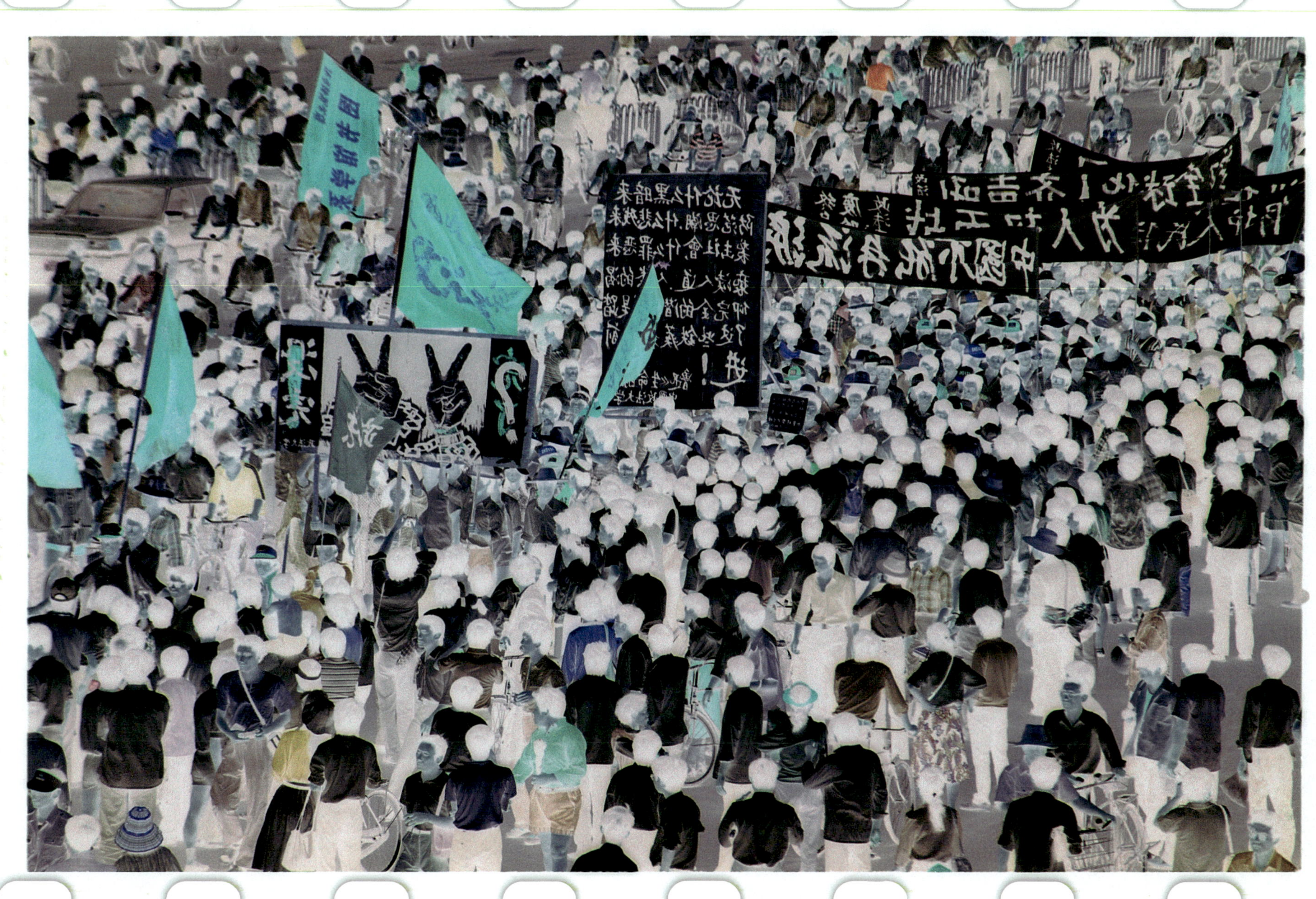

11

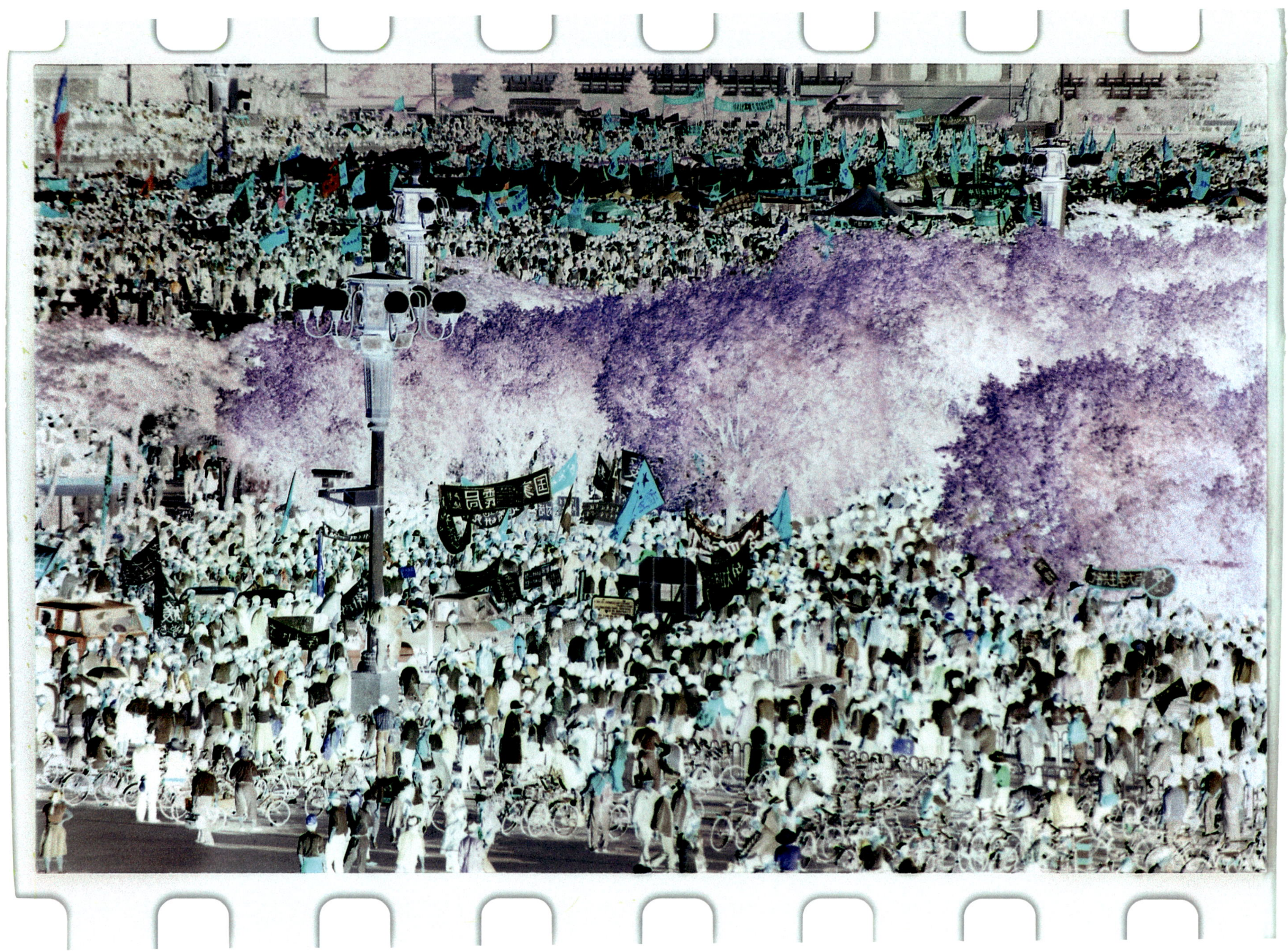

13

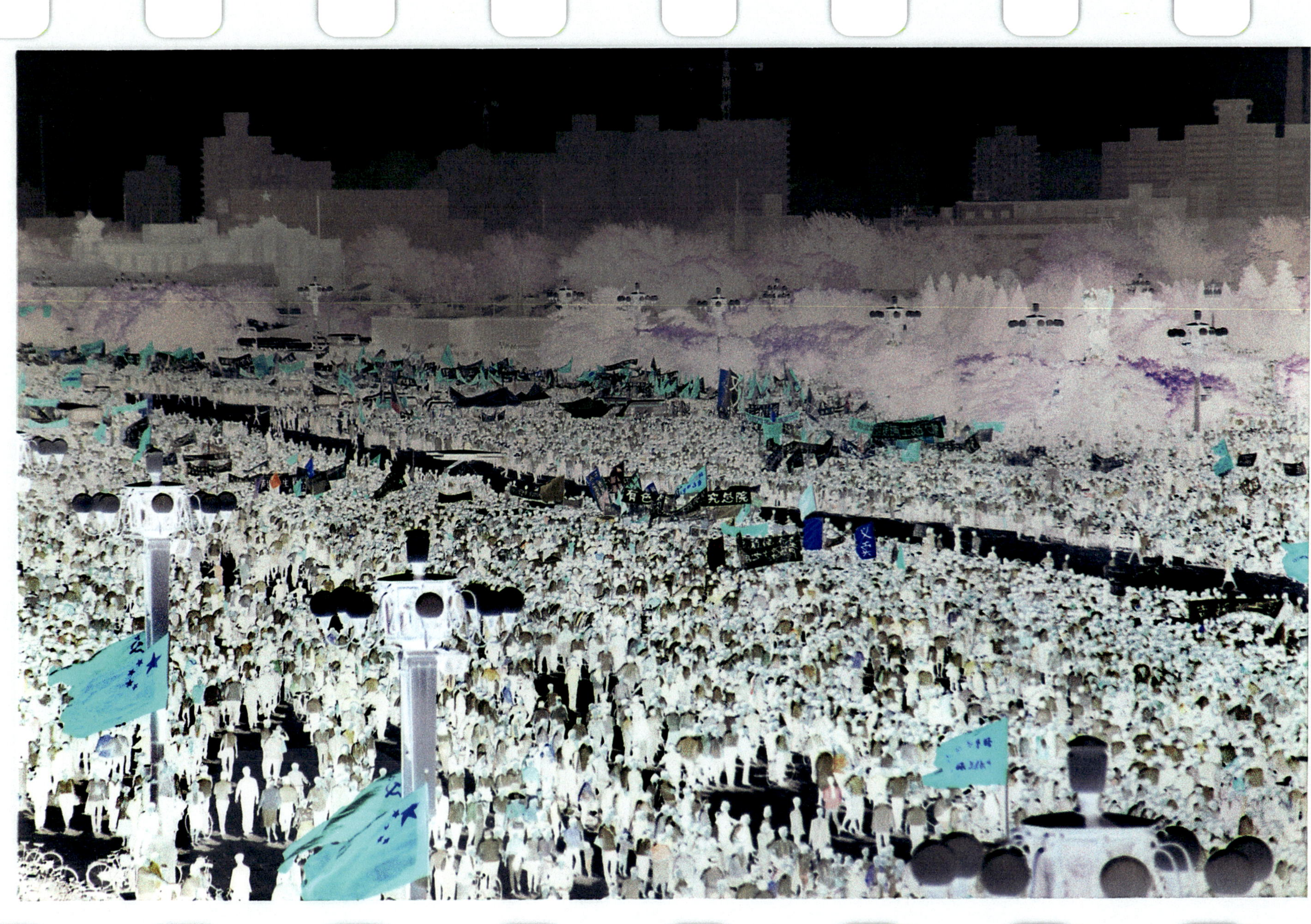

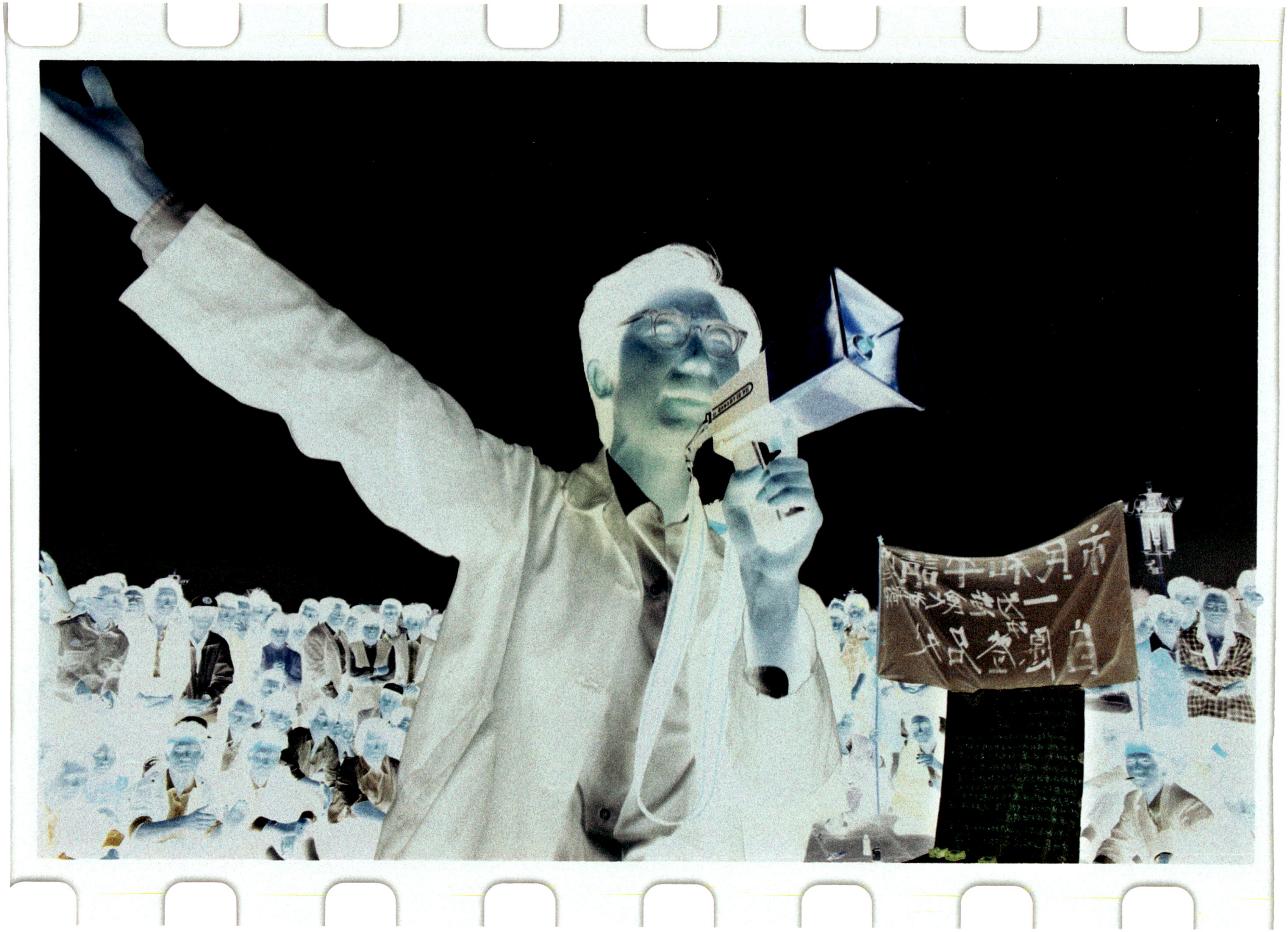

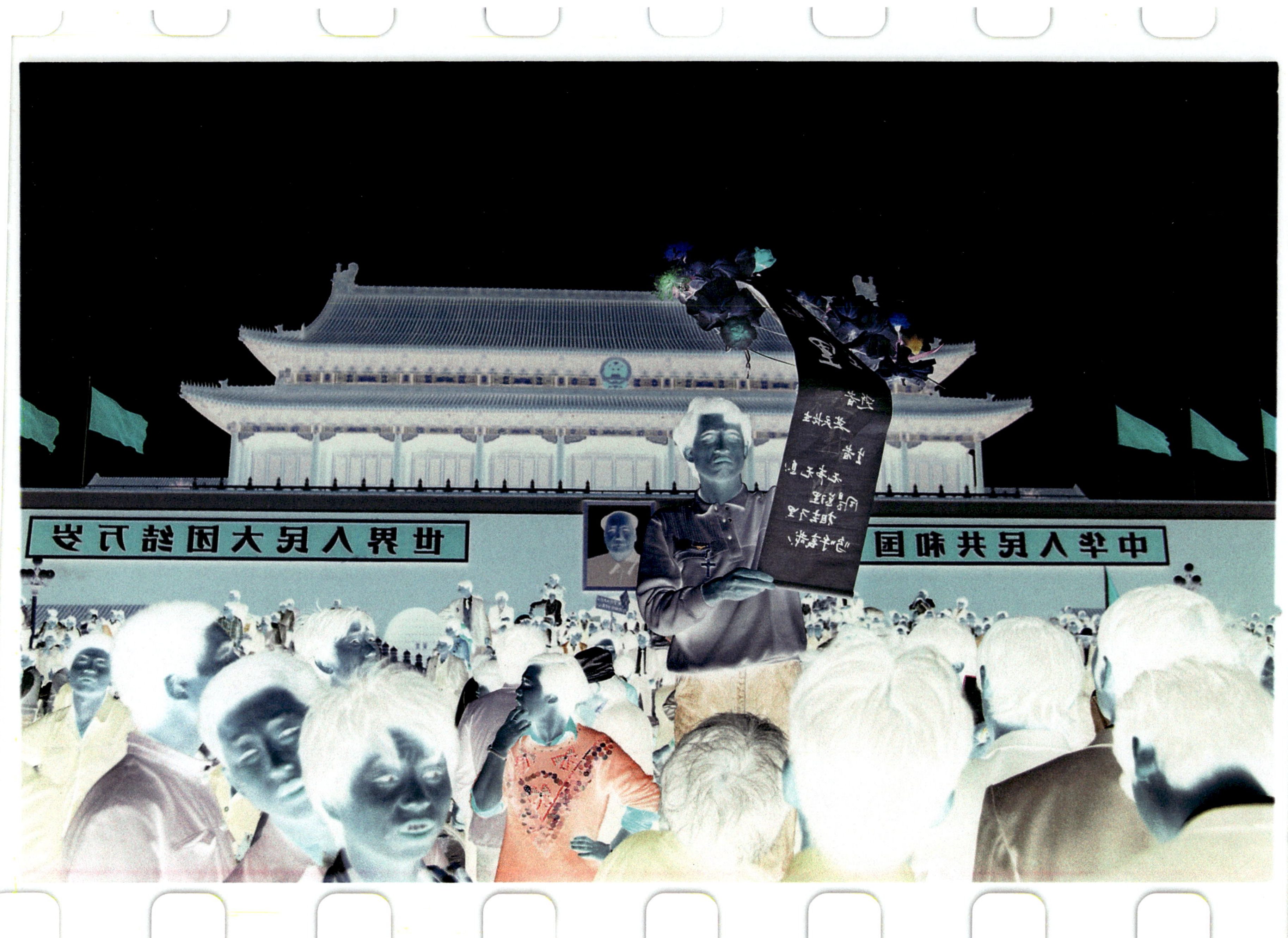

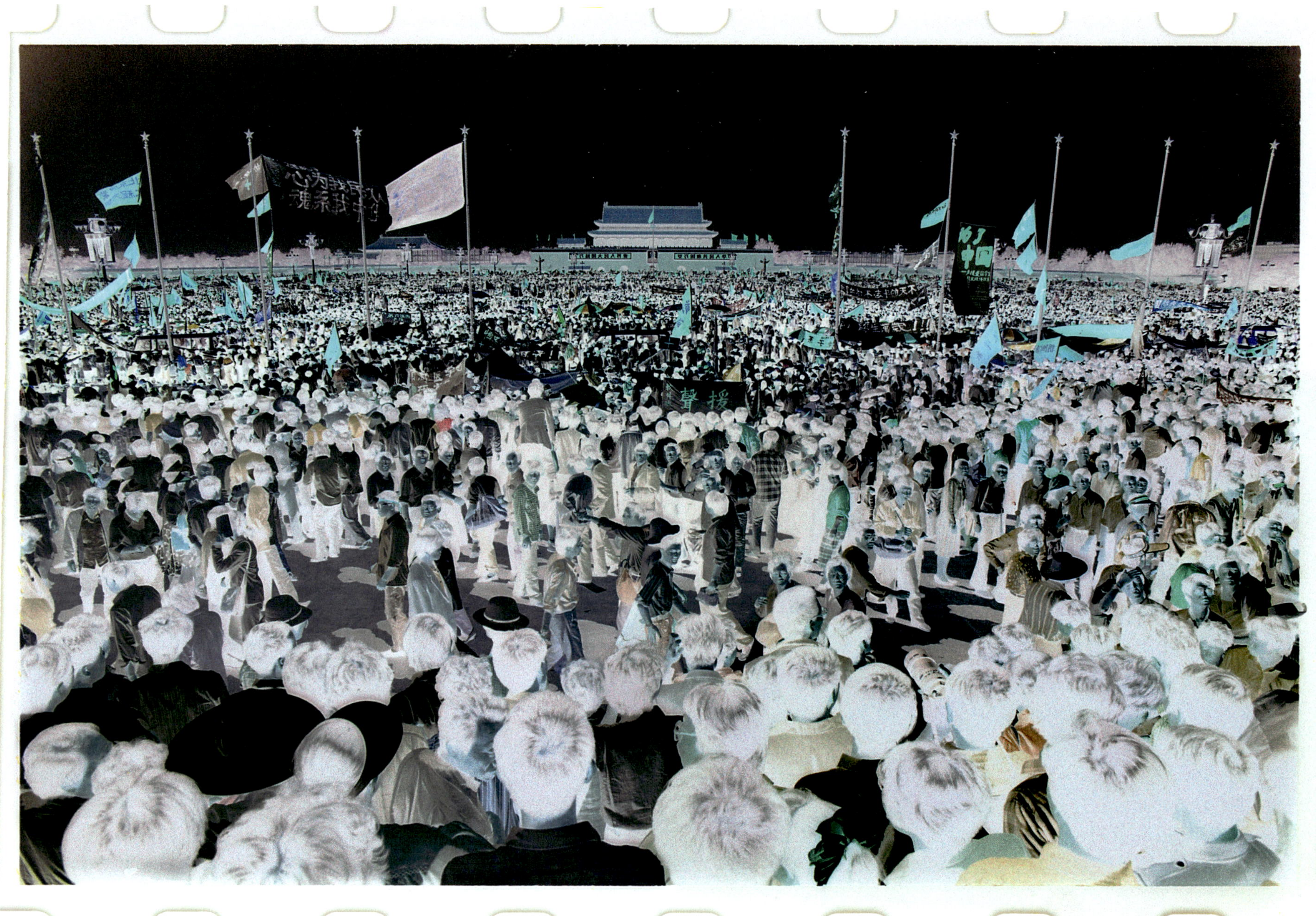

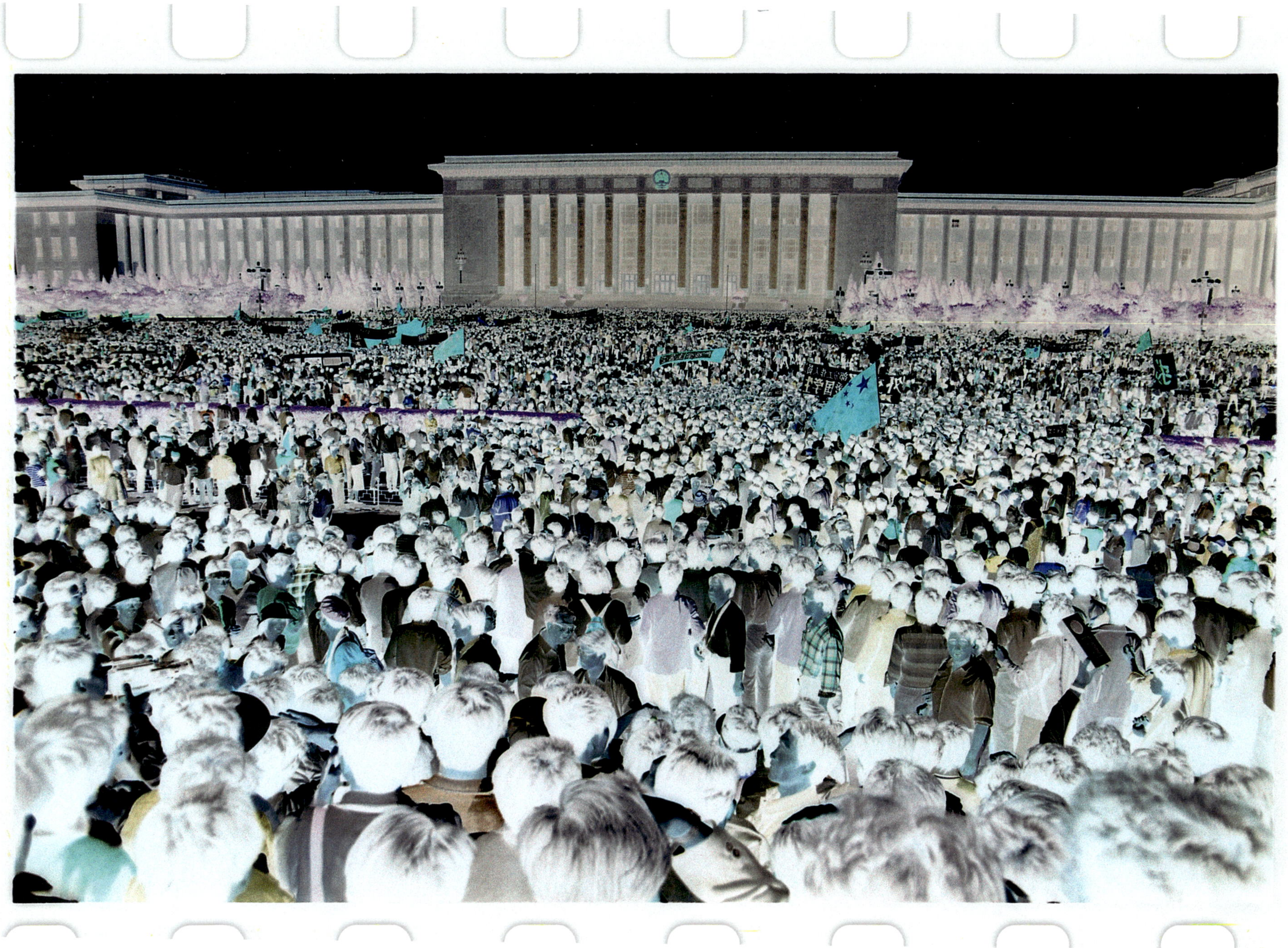

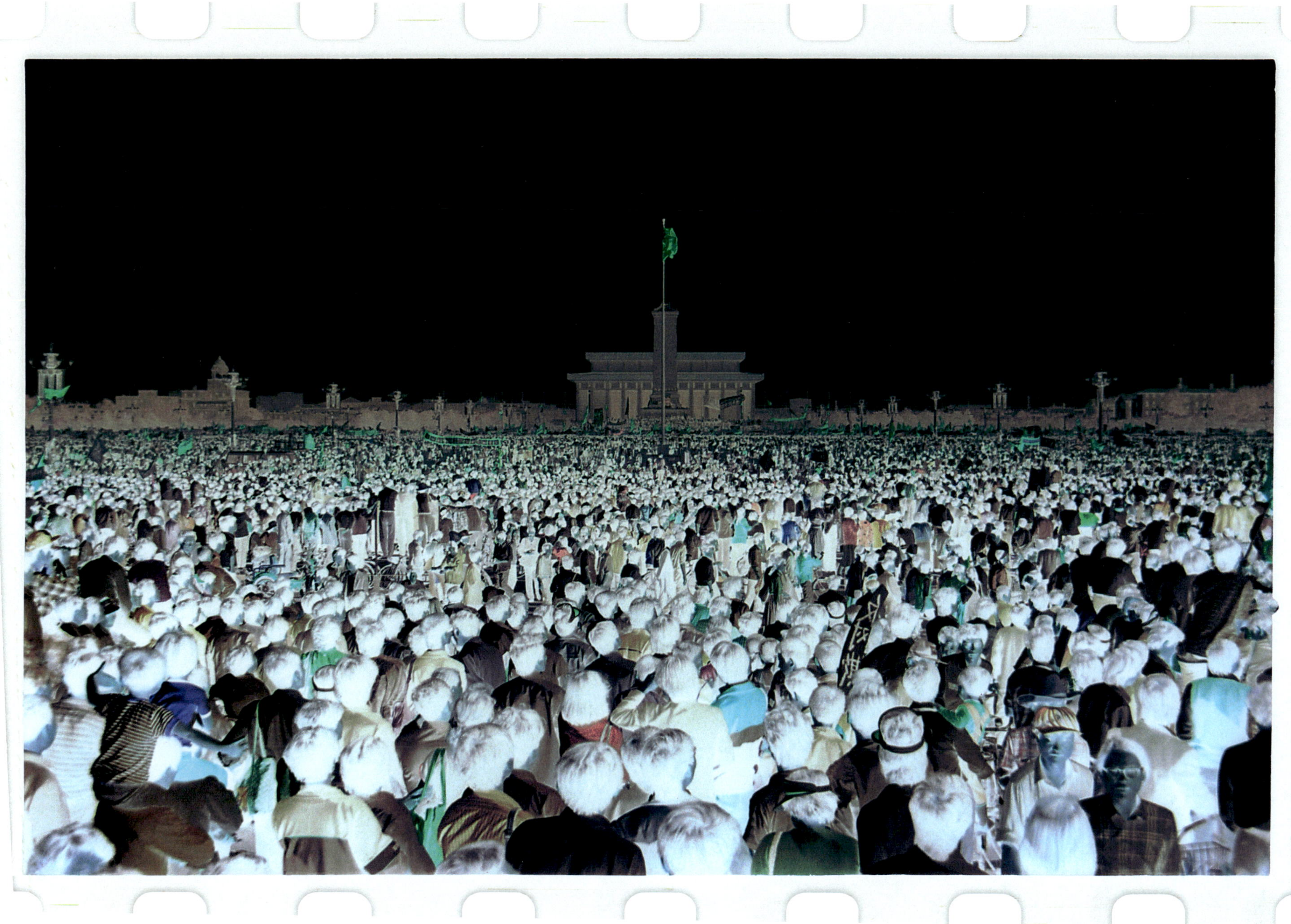

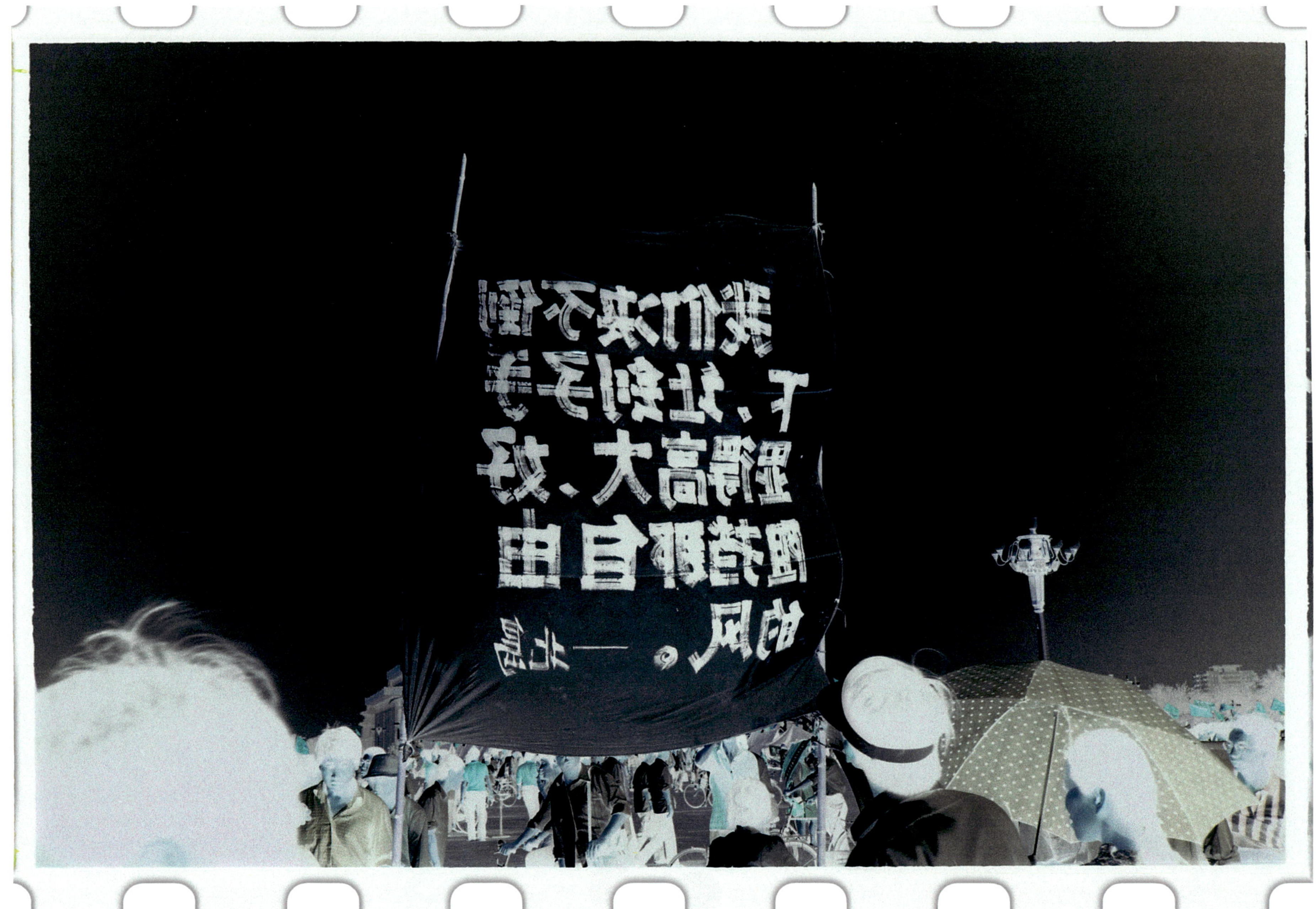

20

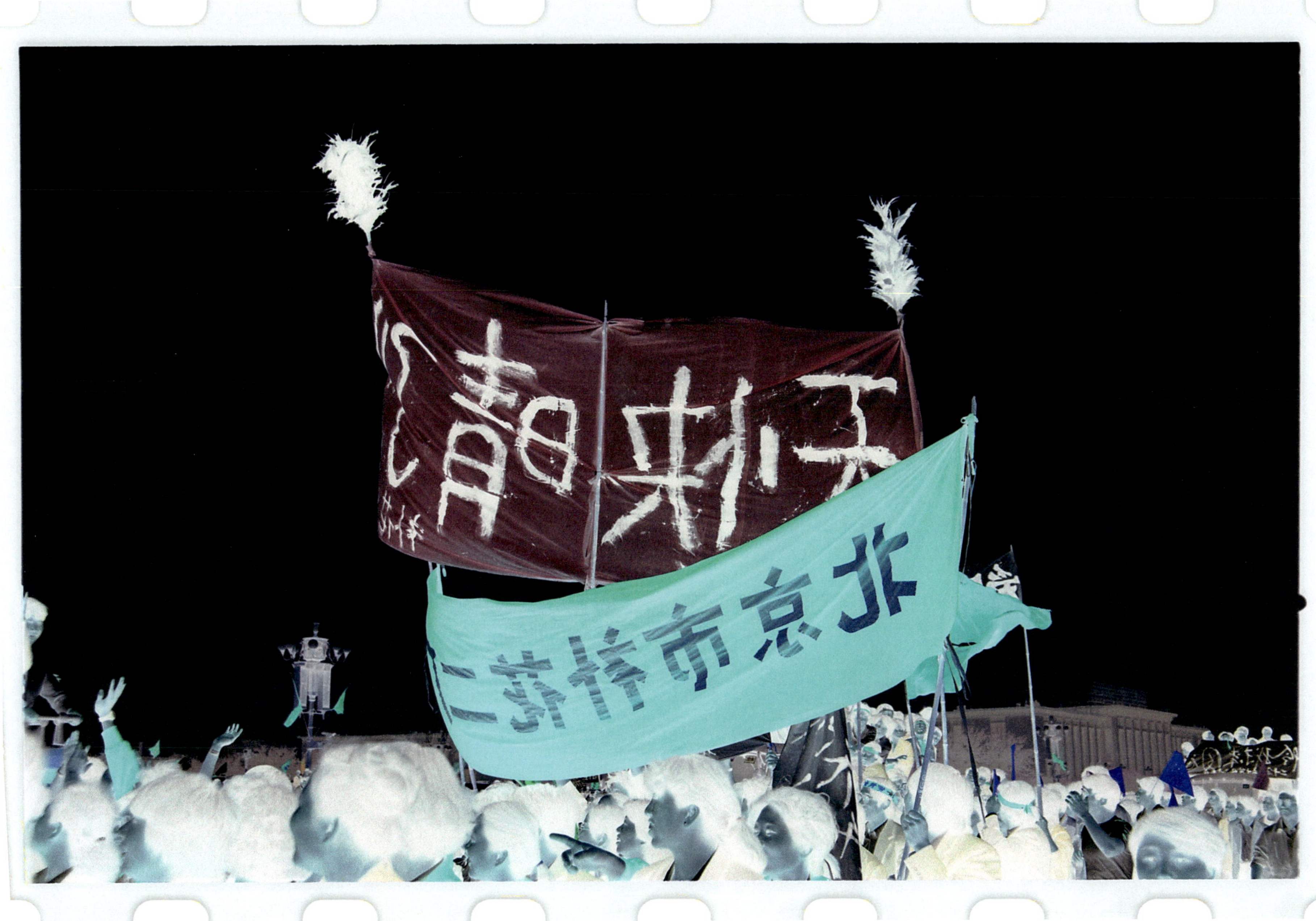

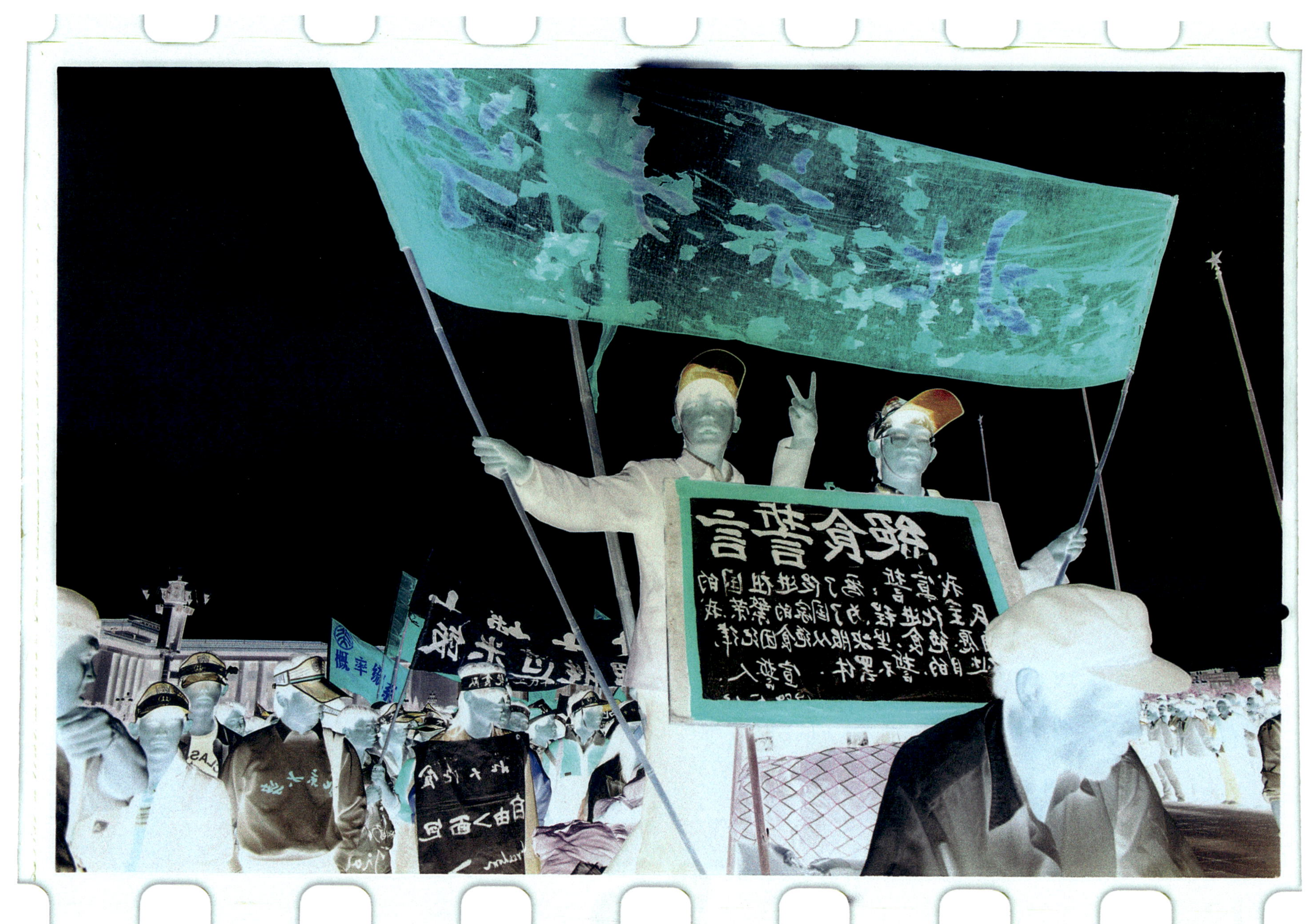

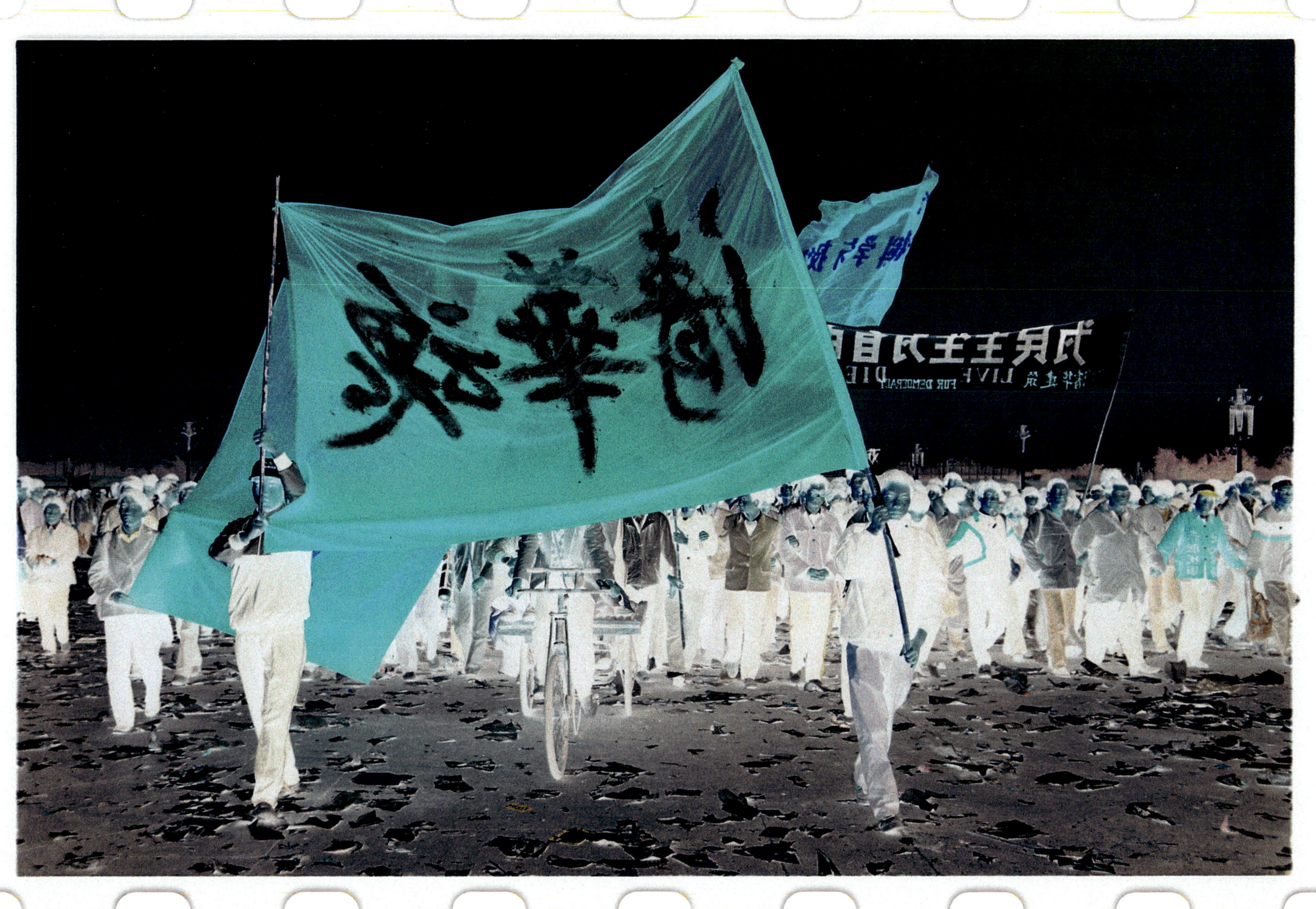

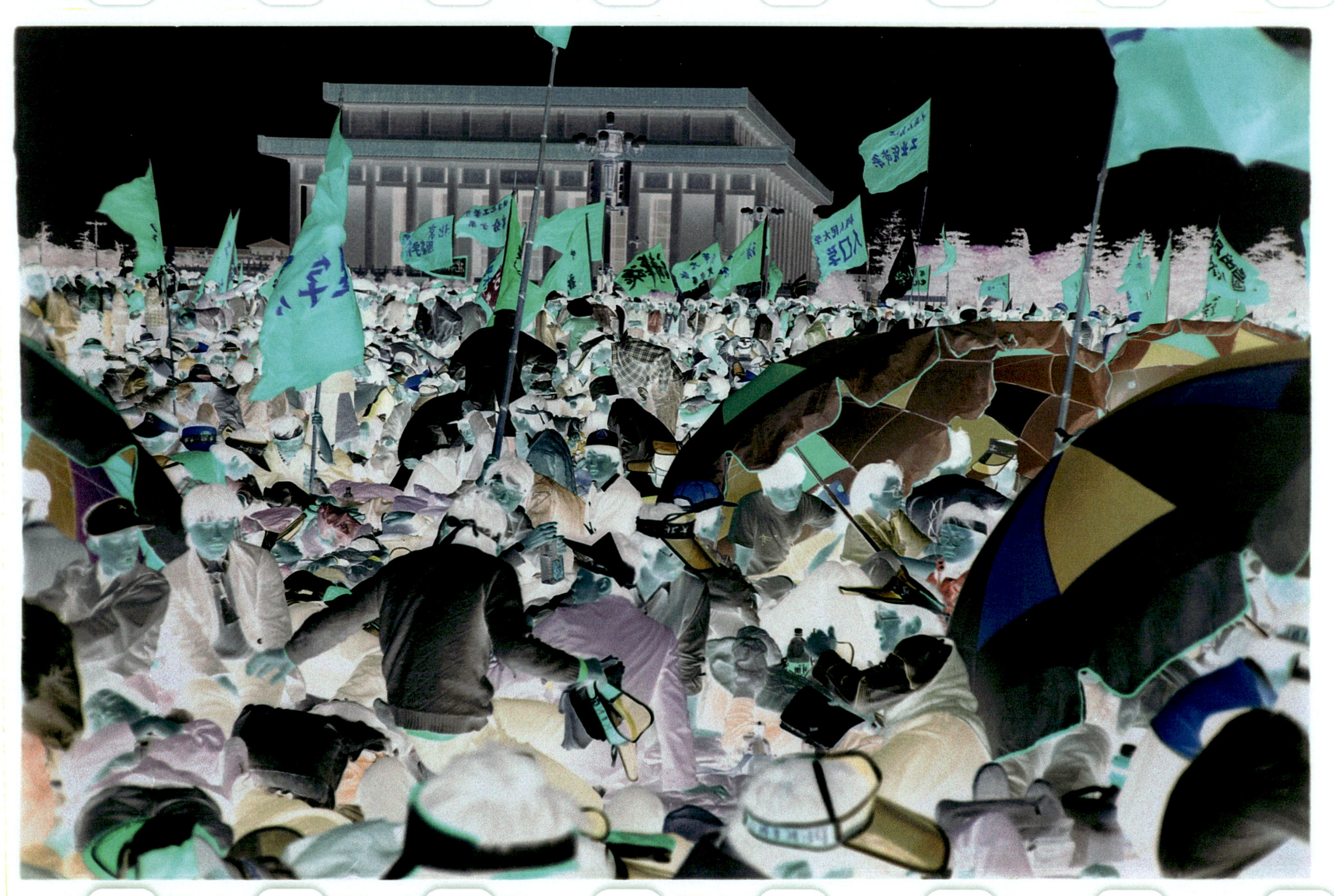

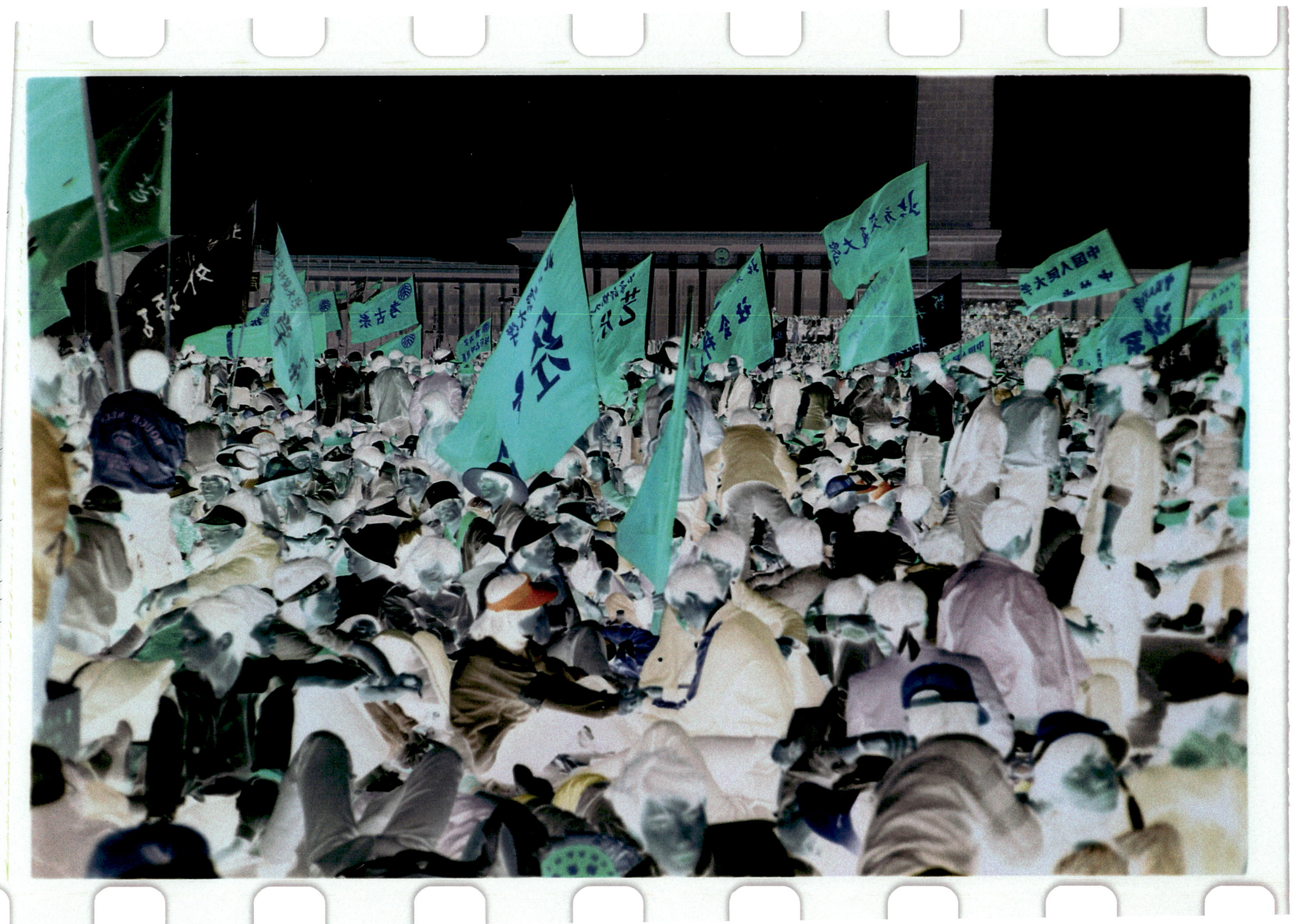

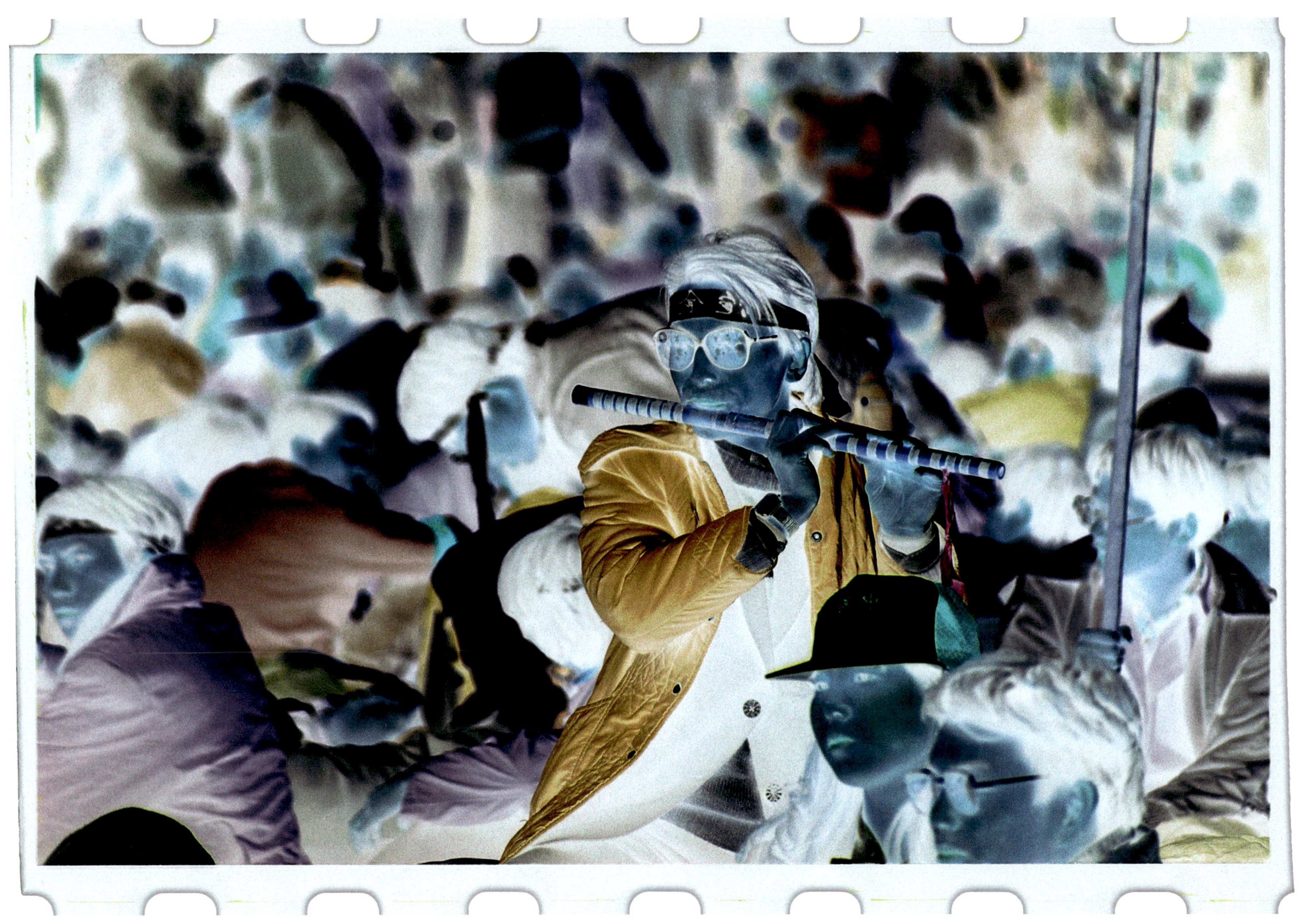

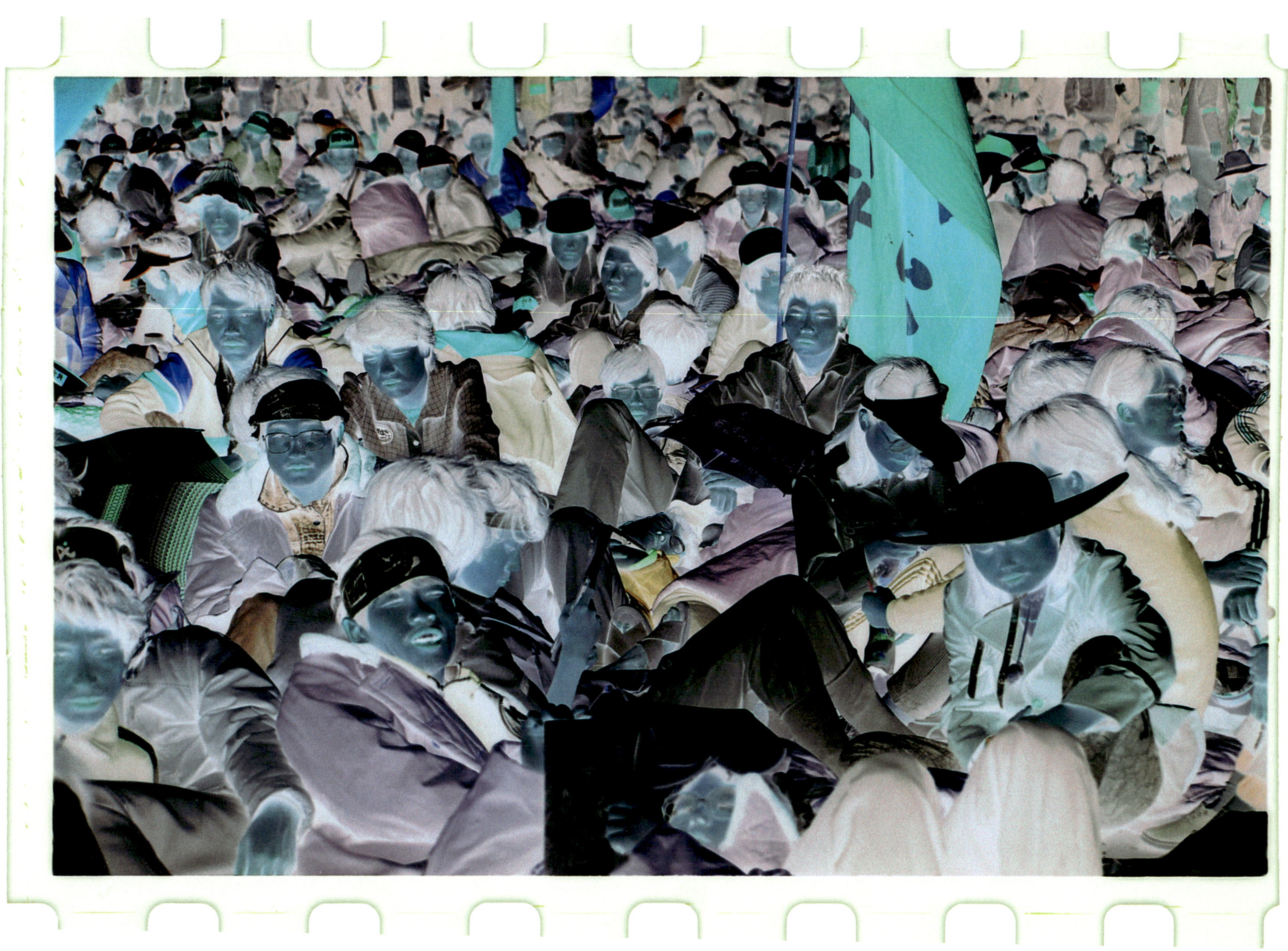

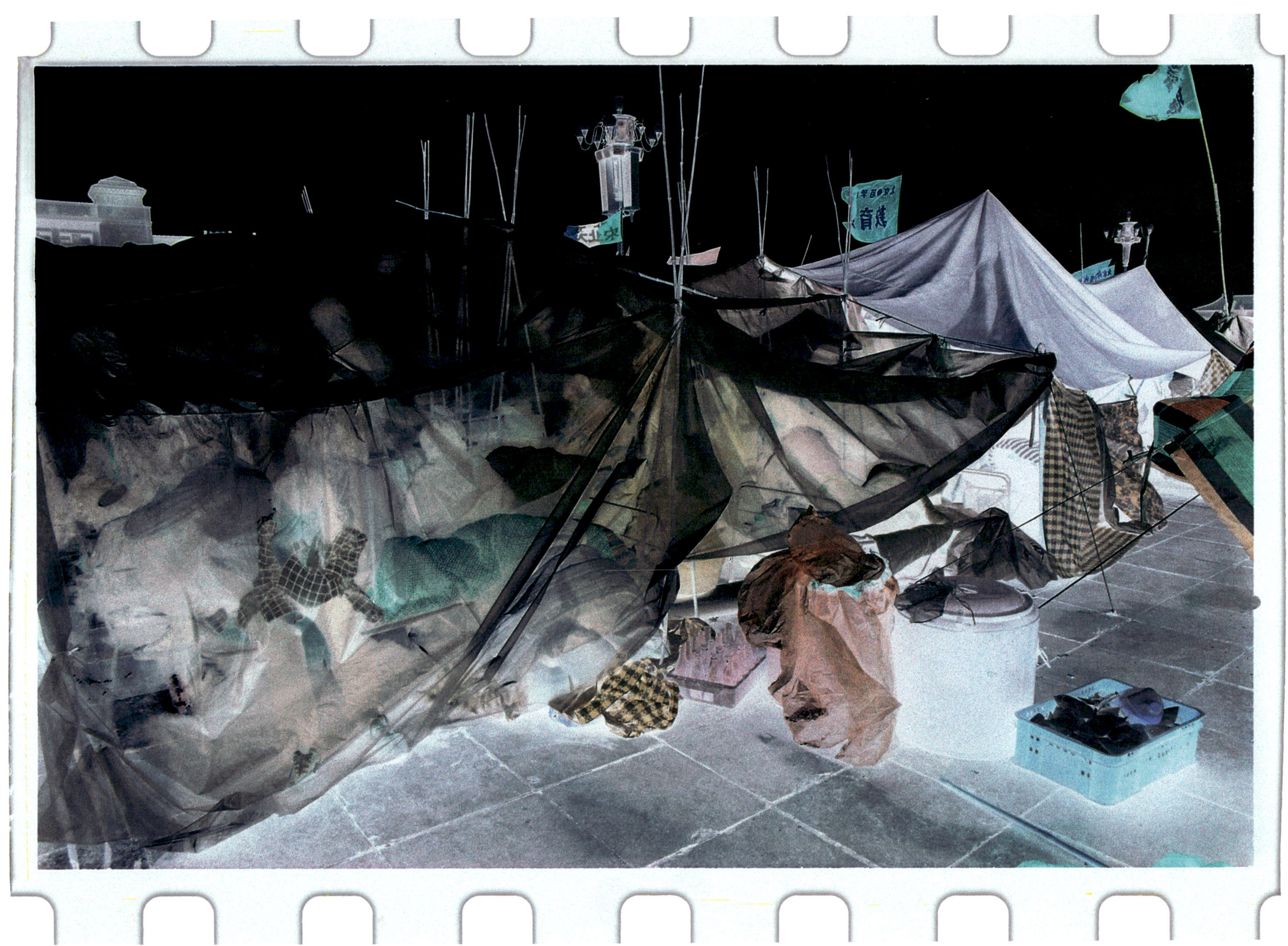

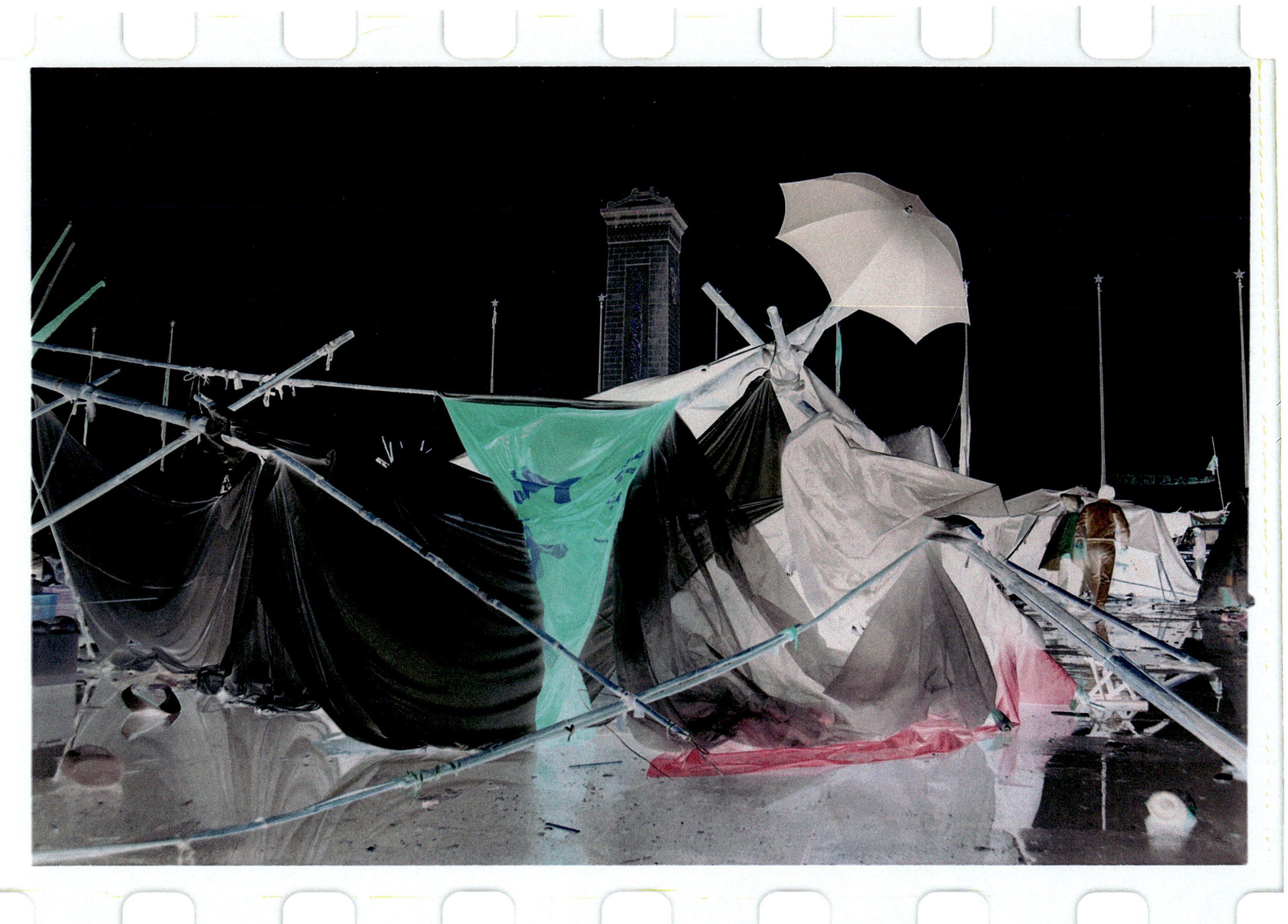

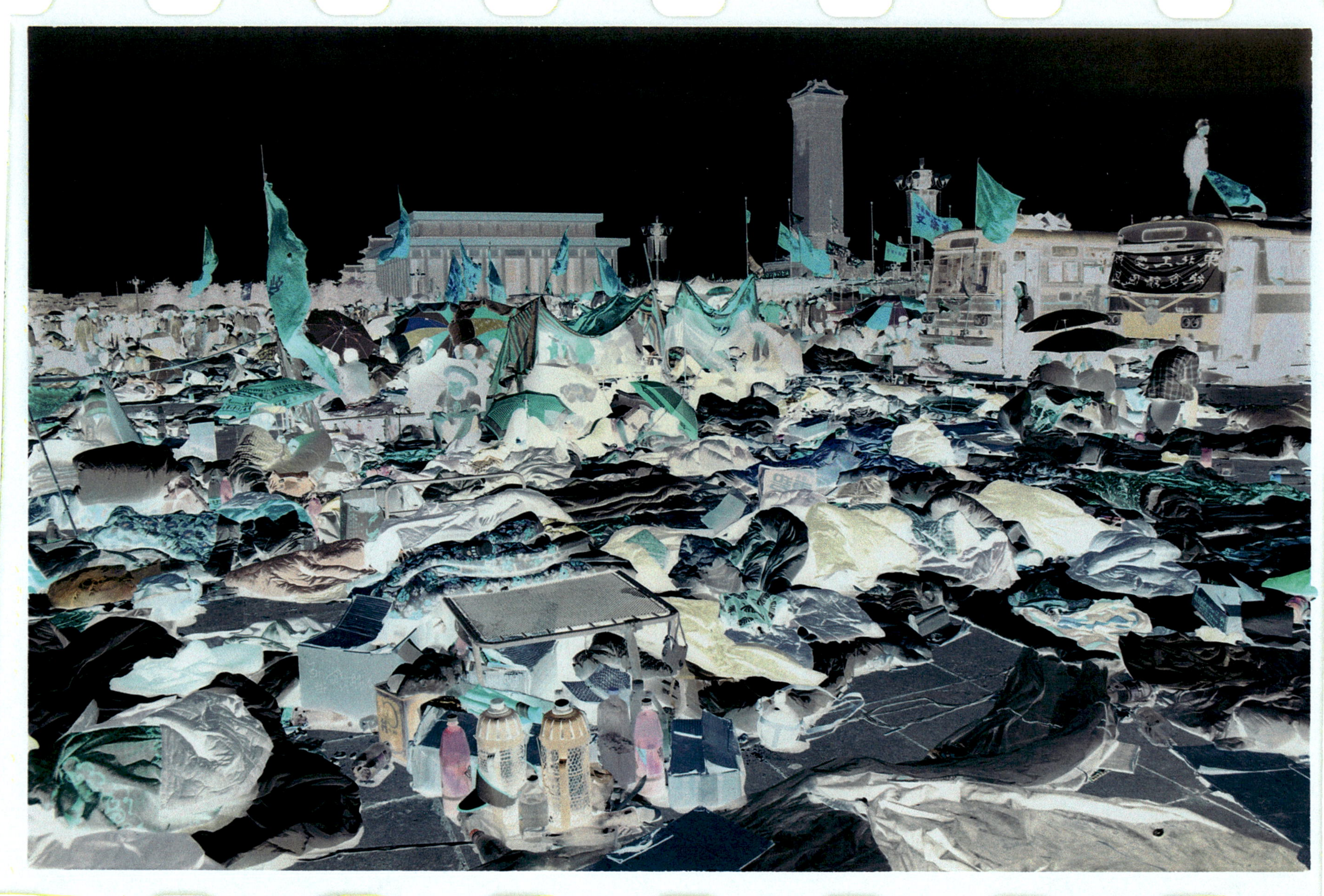

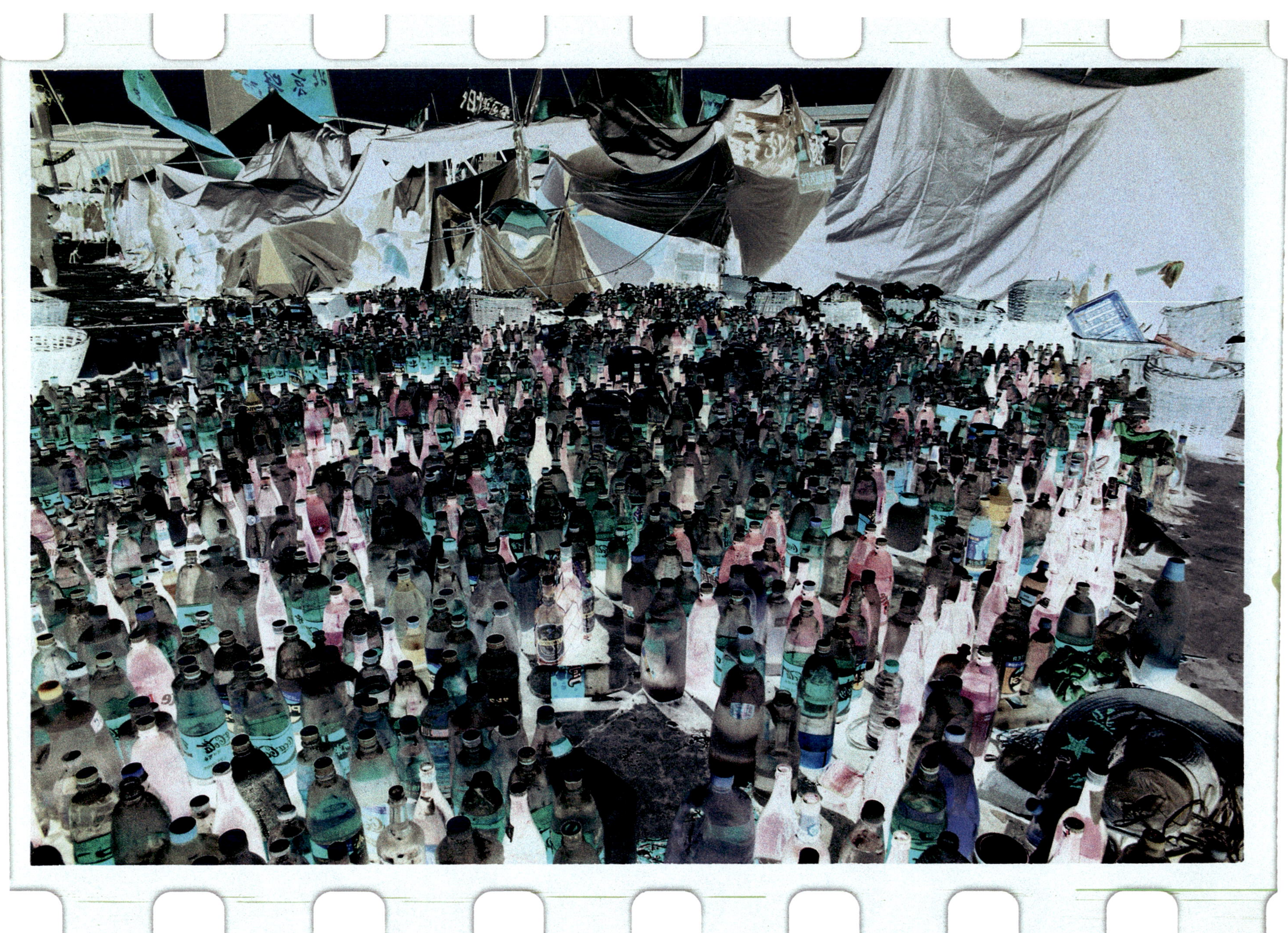

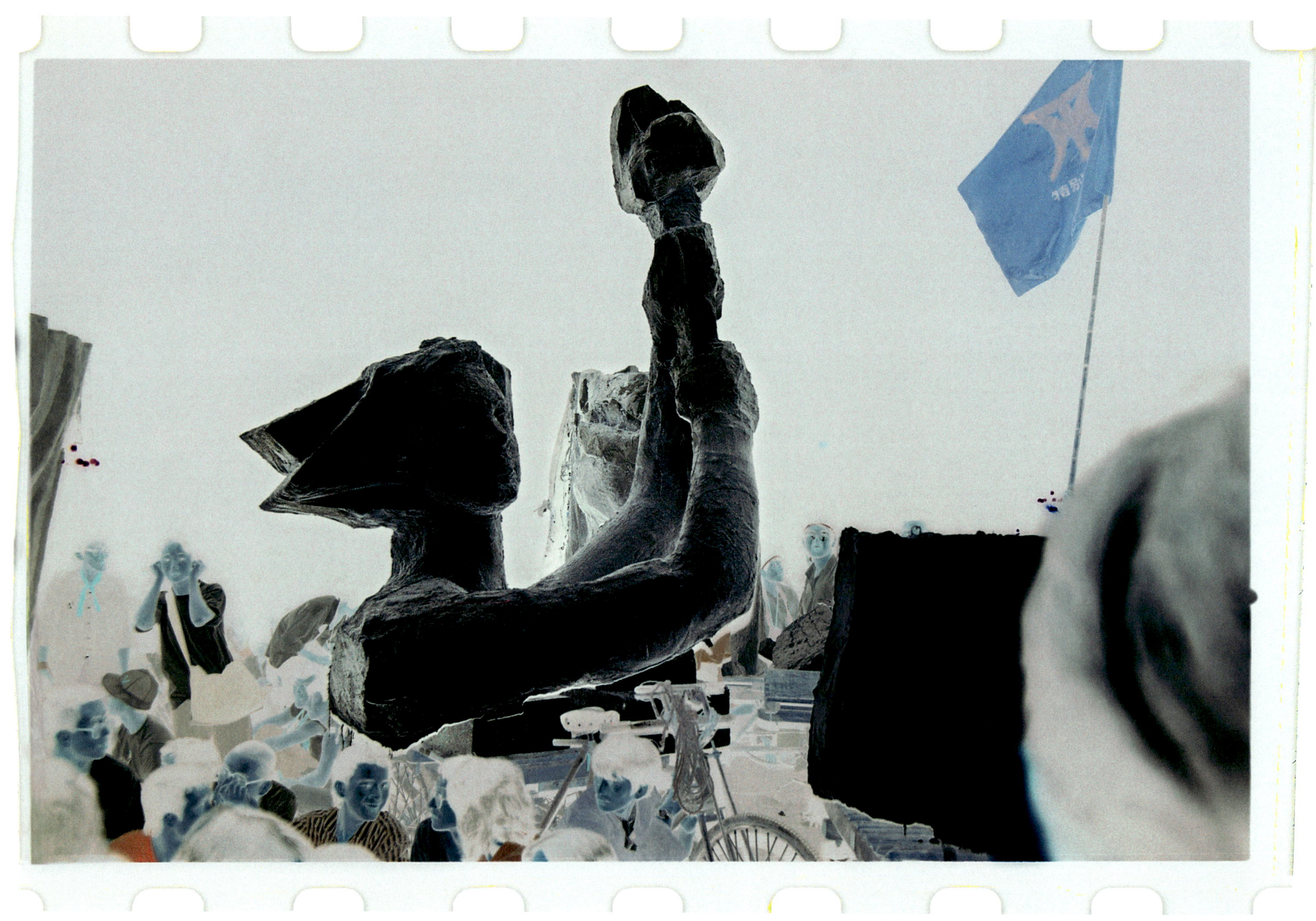

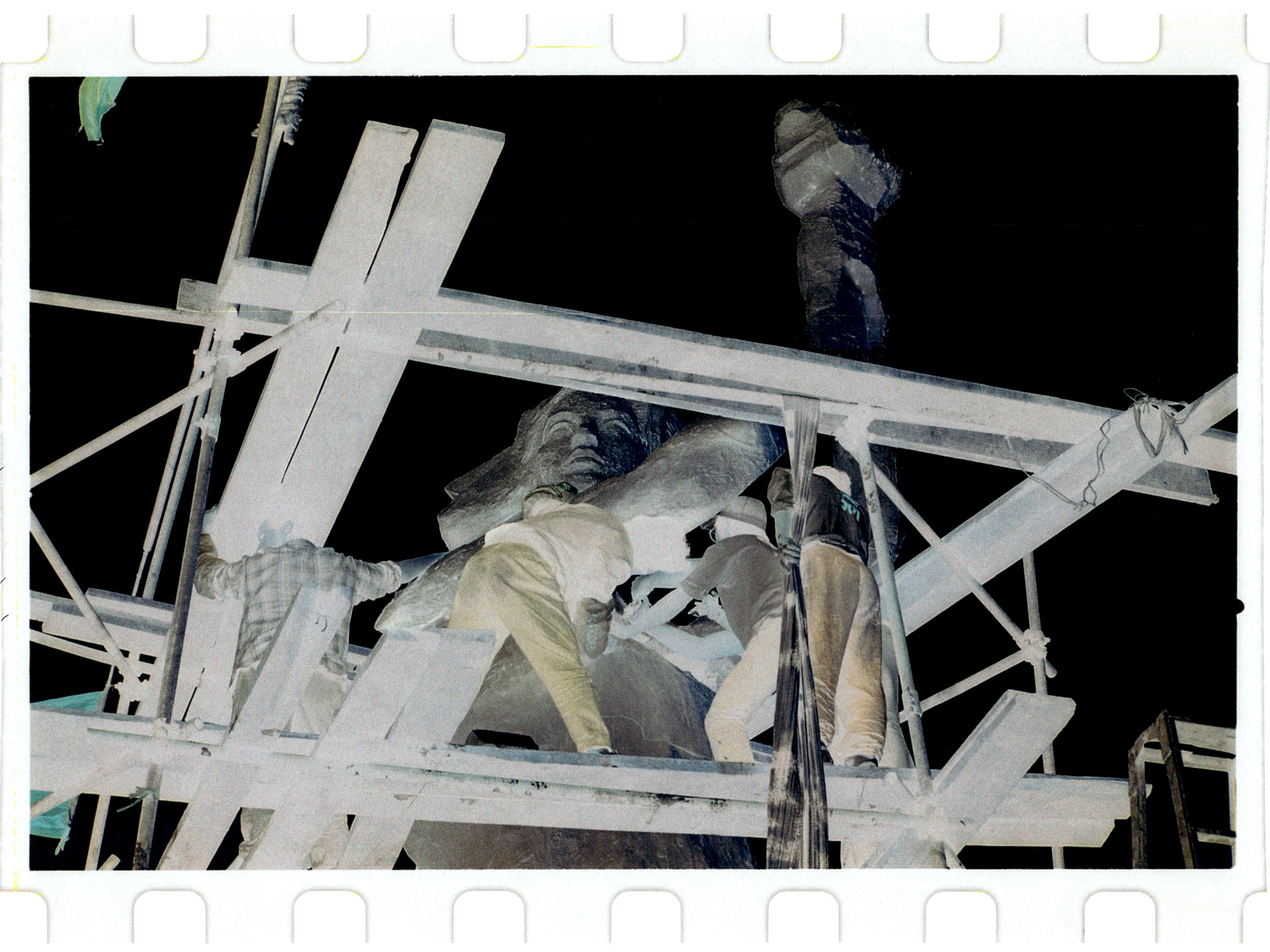

32

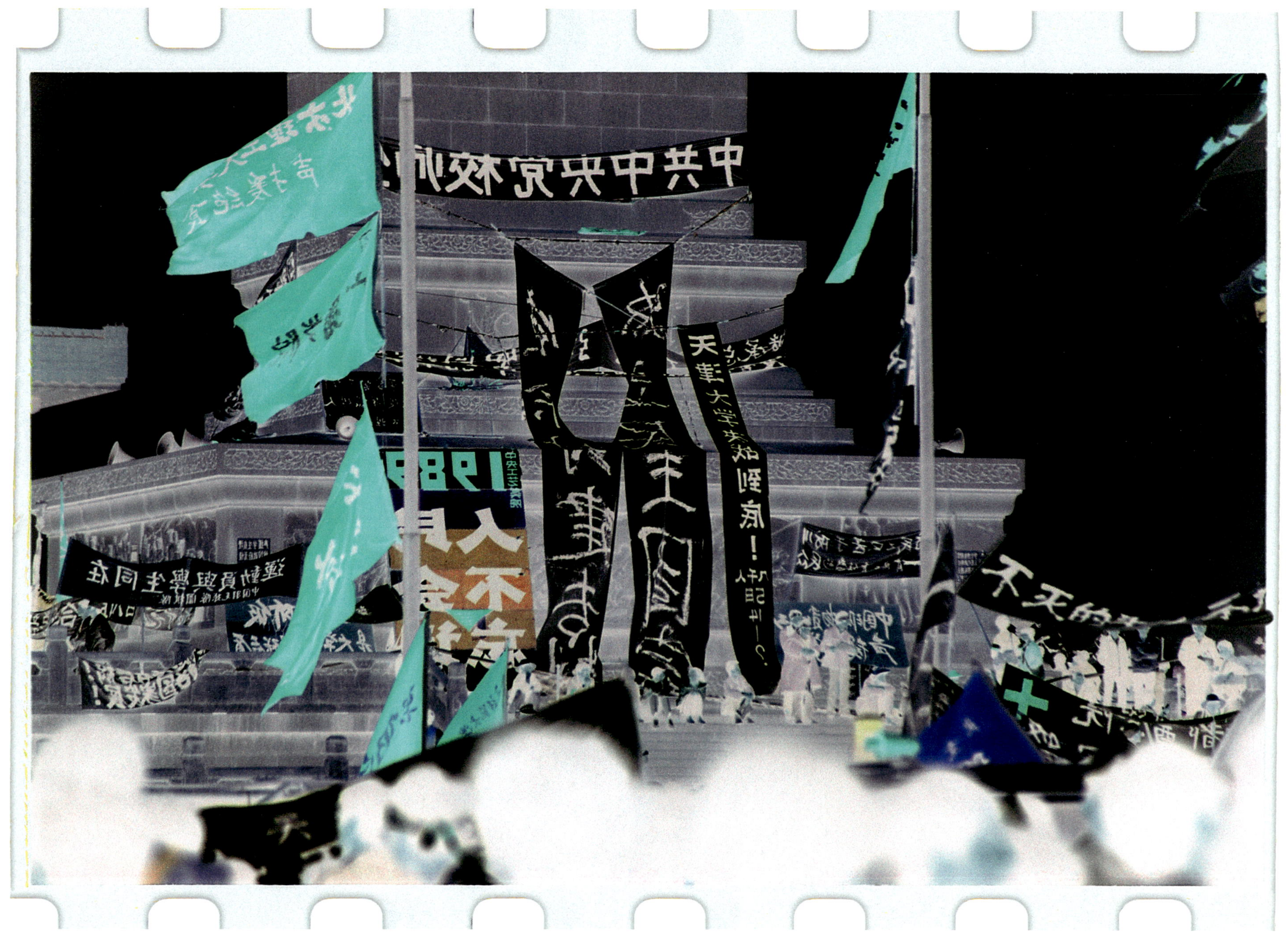

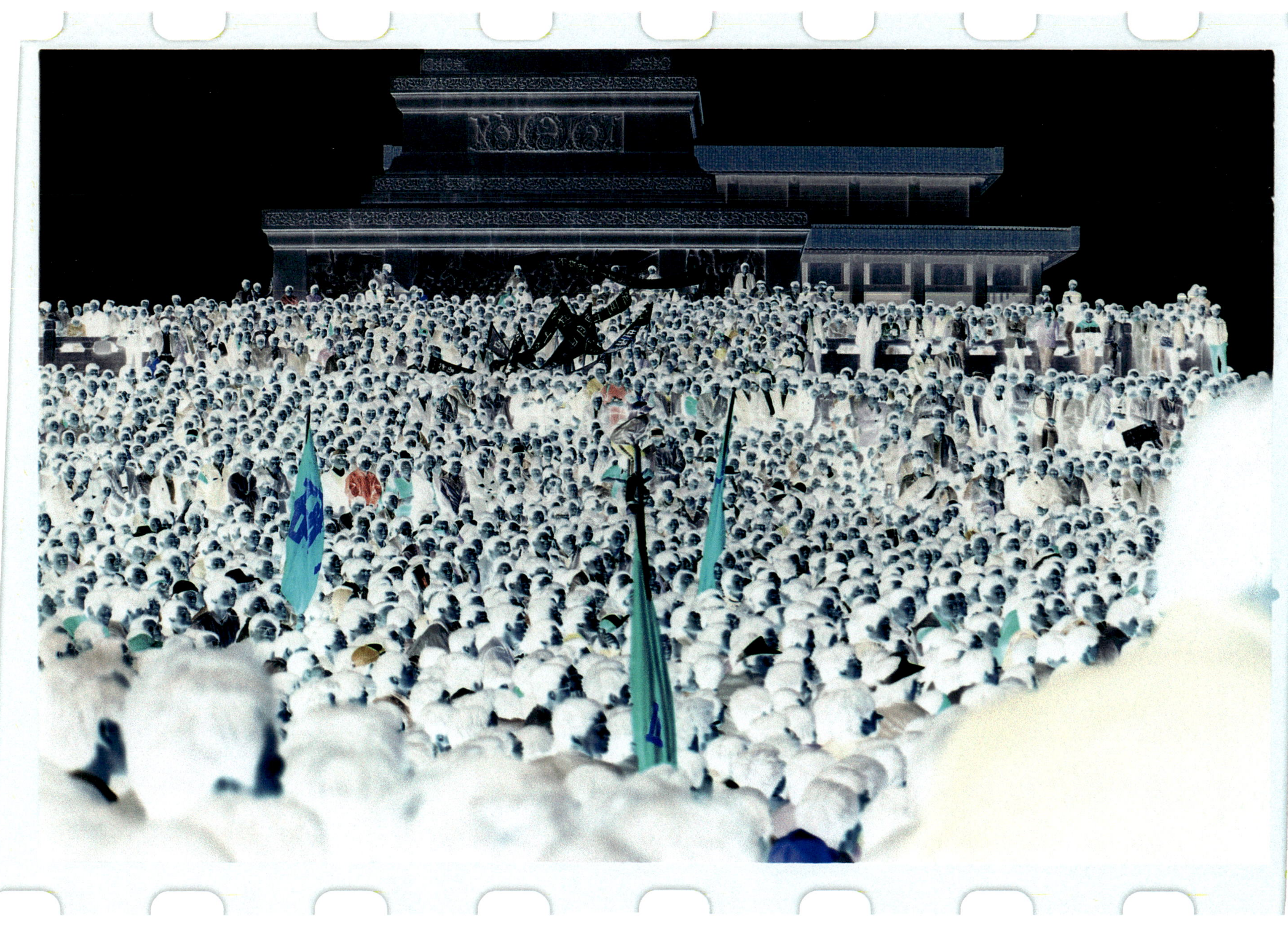

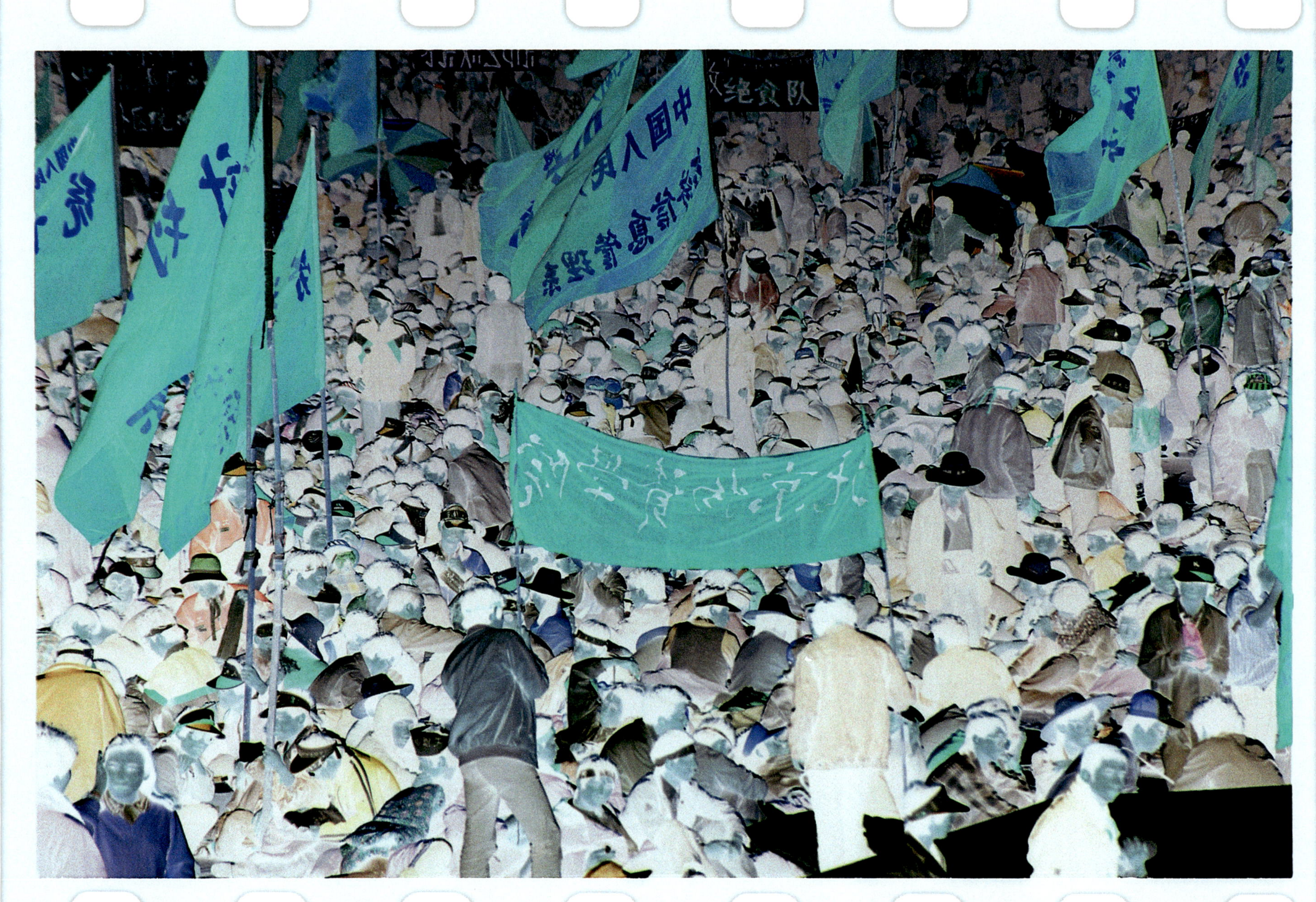

35

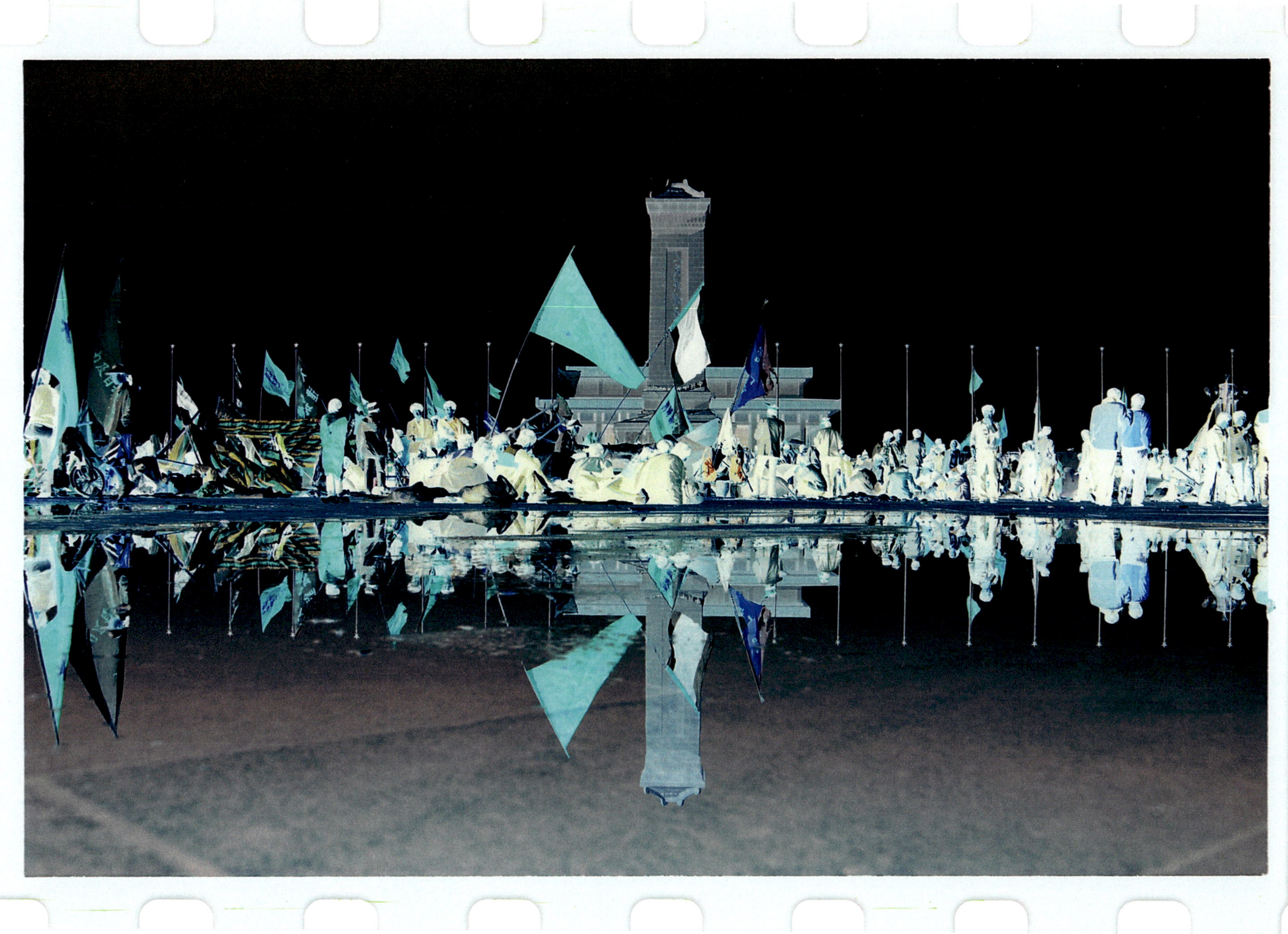

36

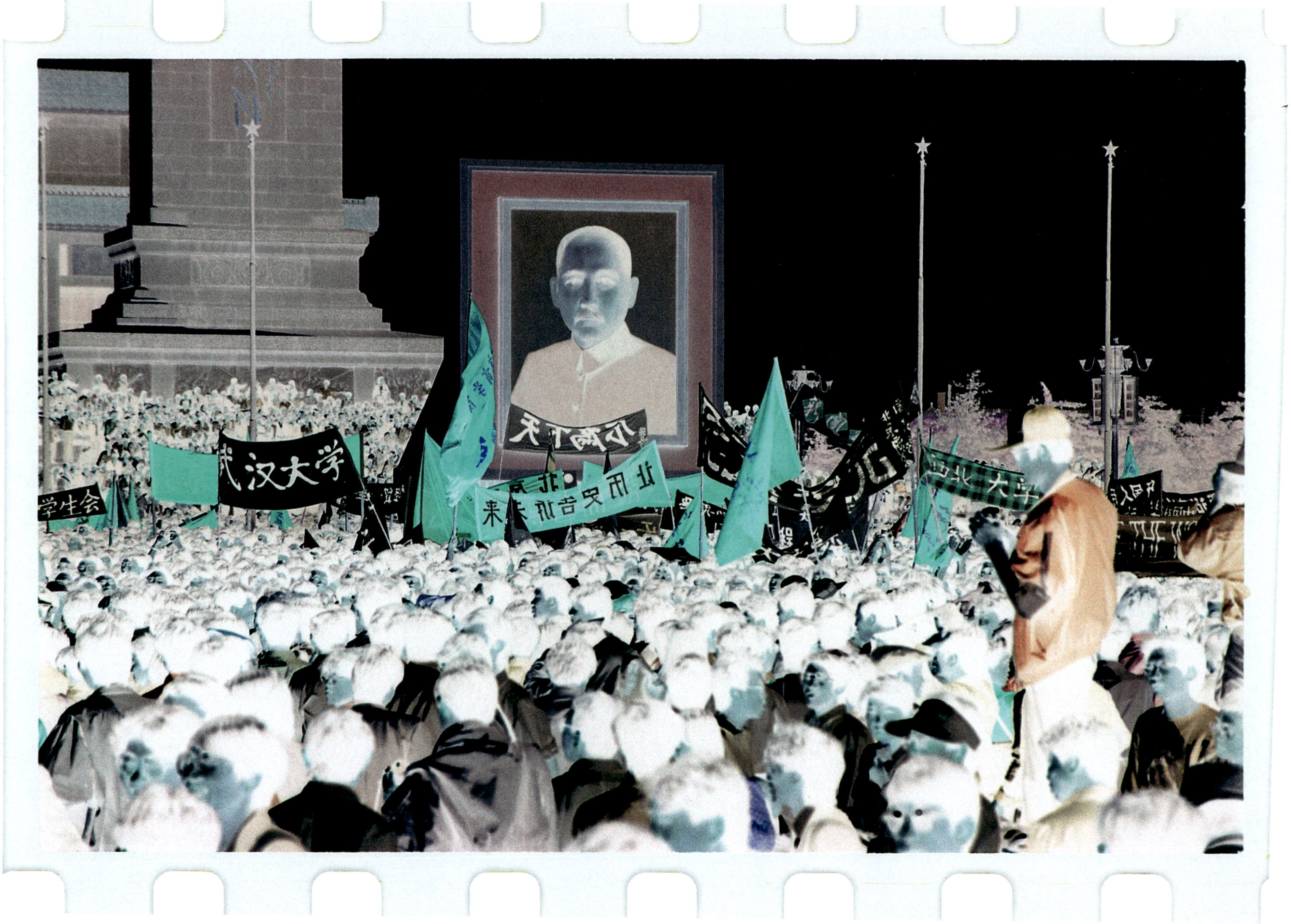

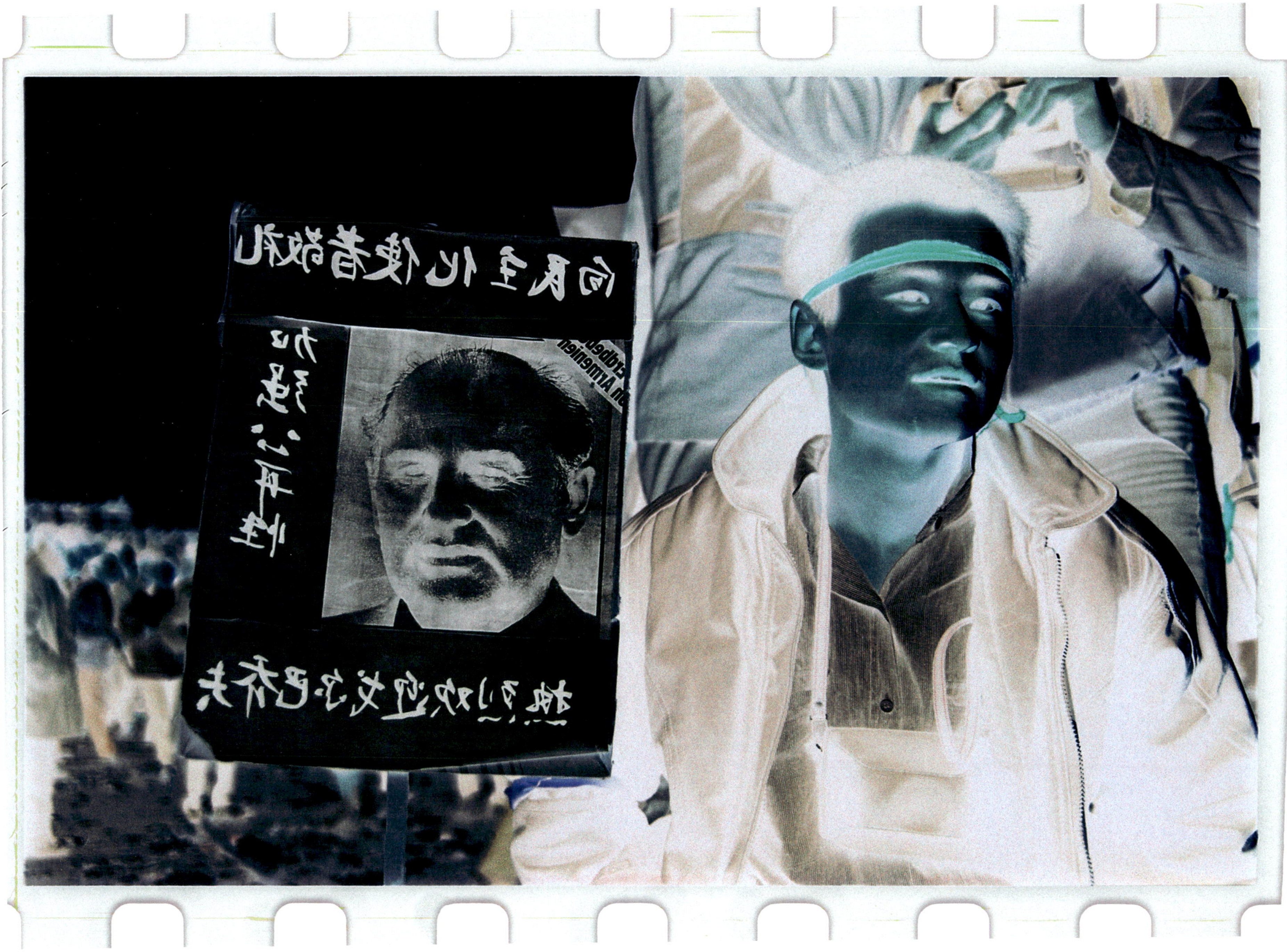

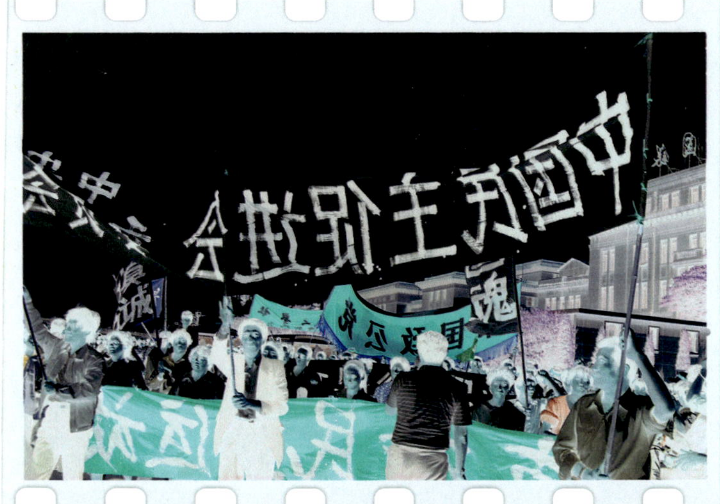 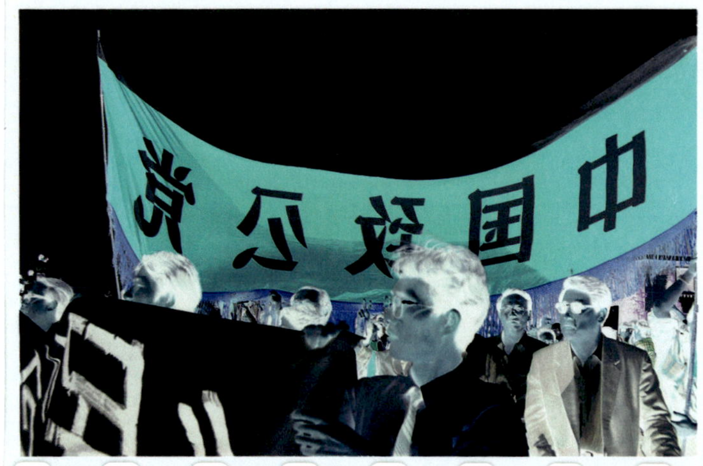 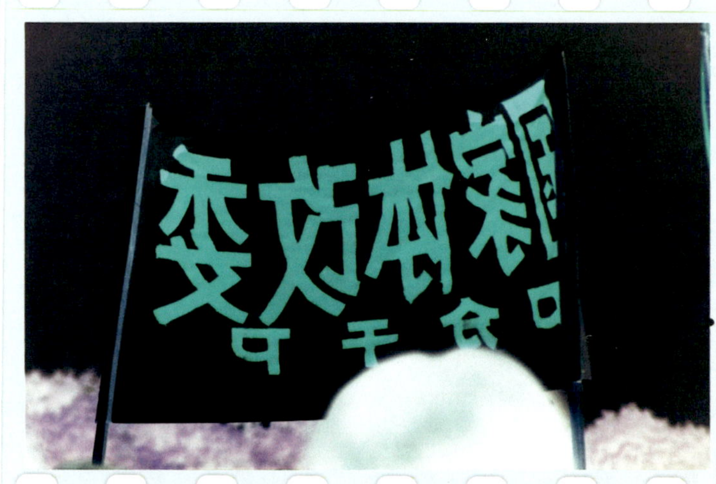

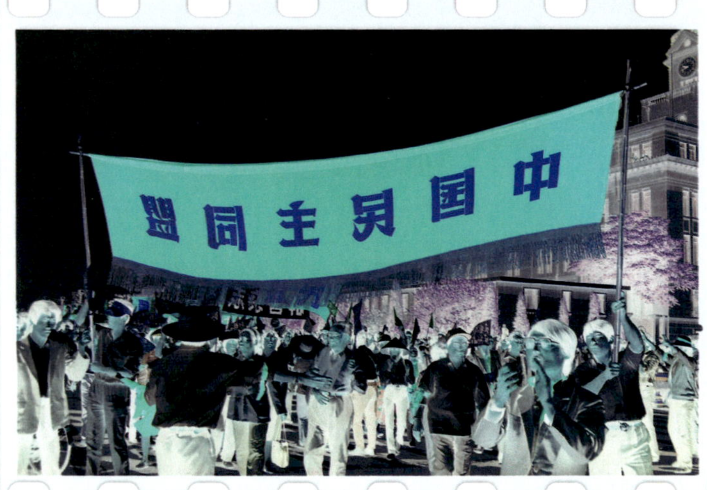 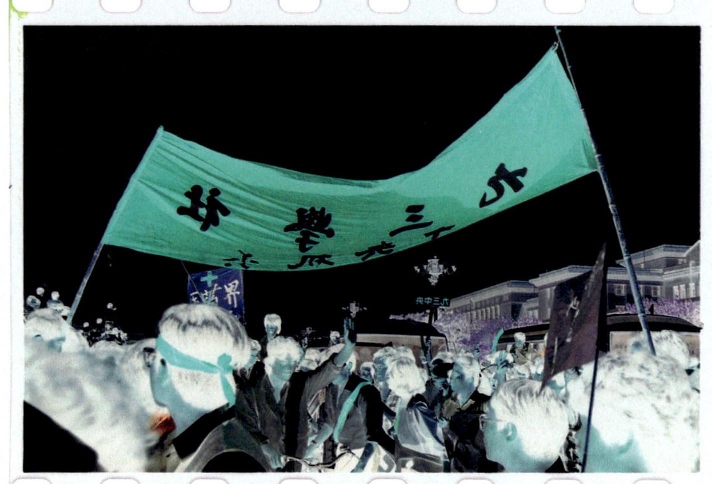 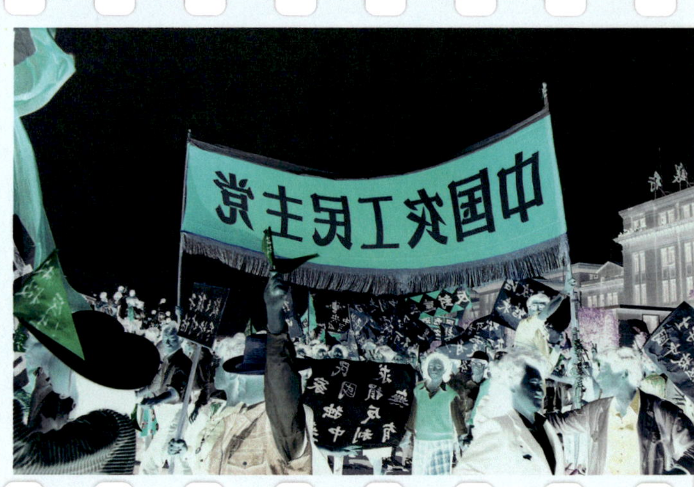

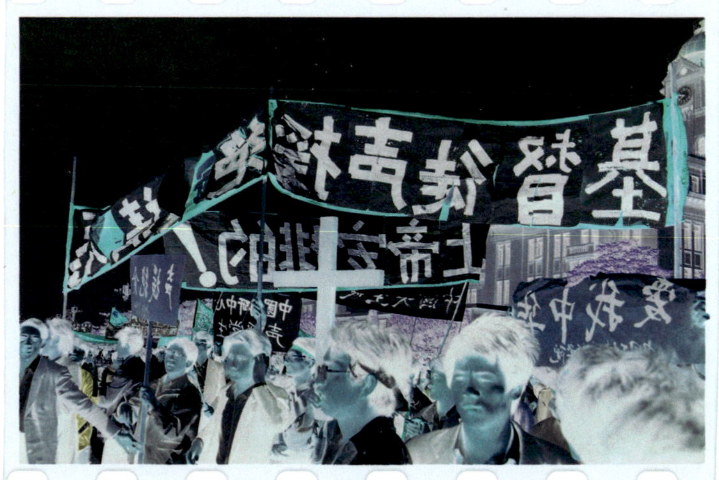
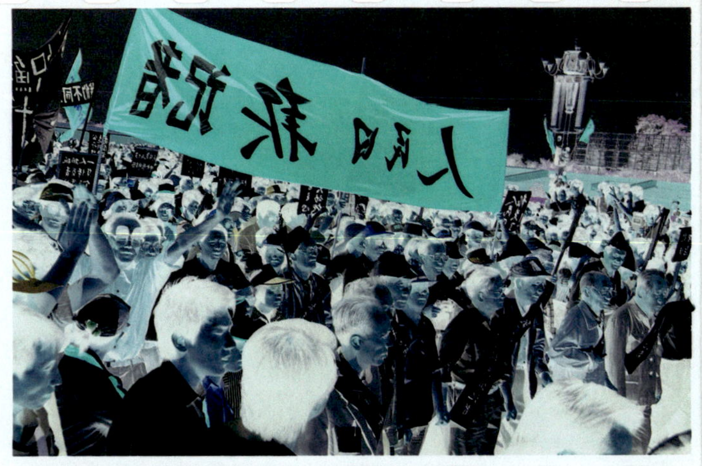
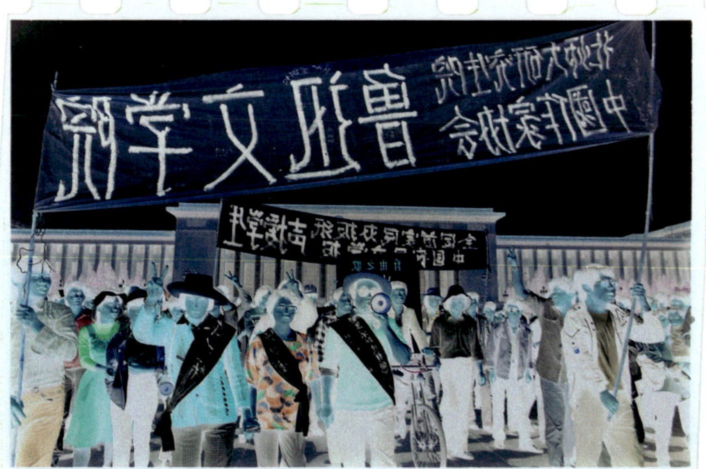
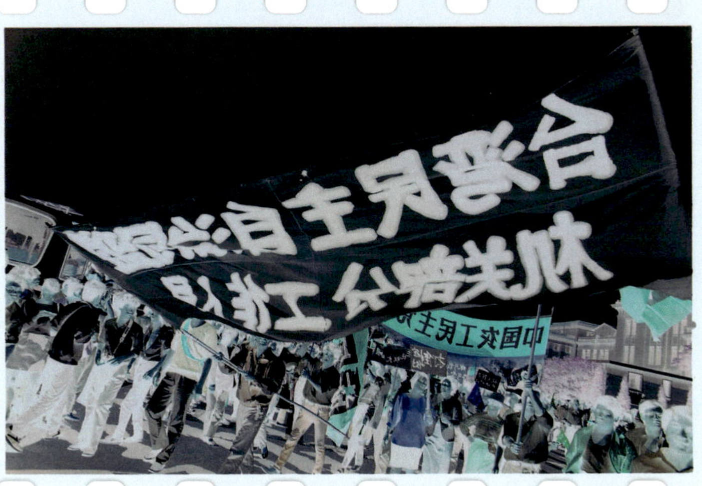
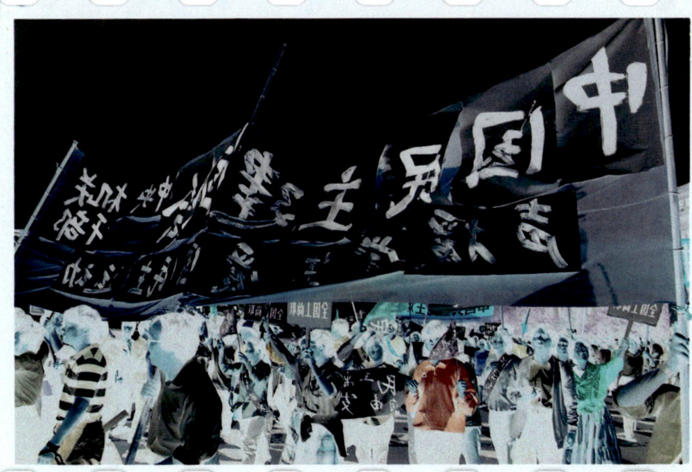
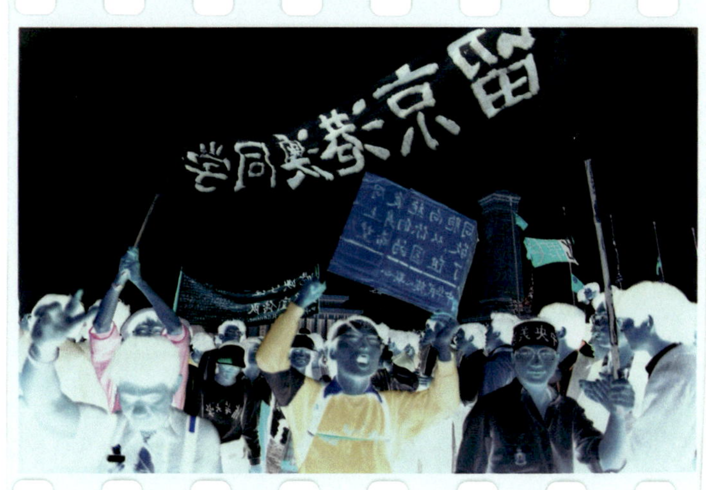

45 —— 50

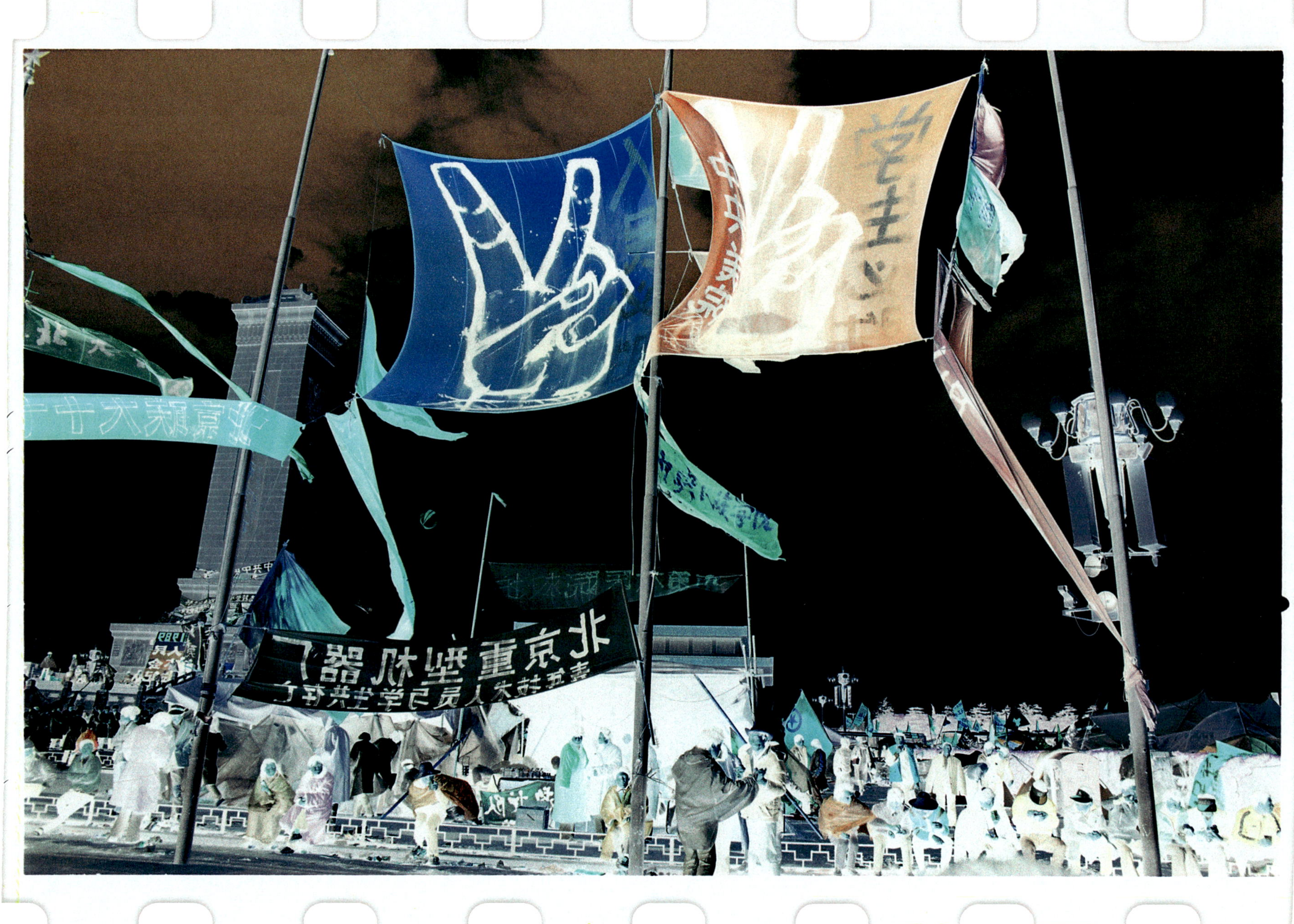

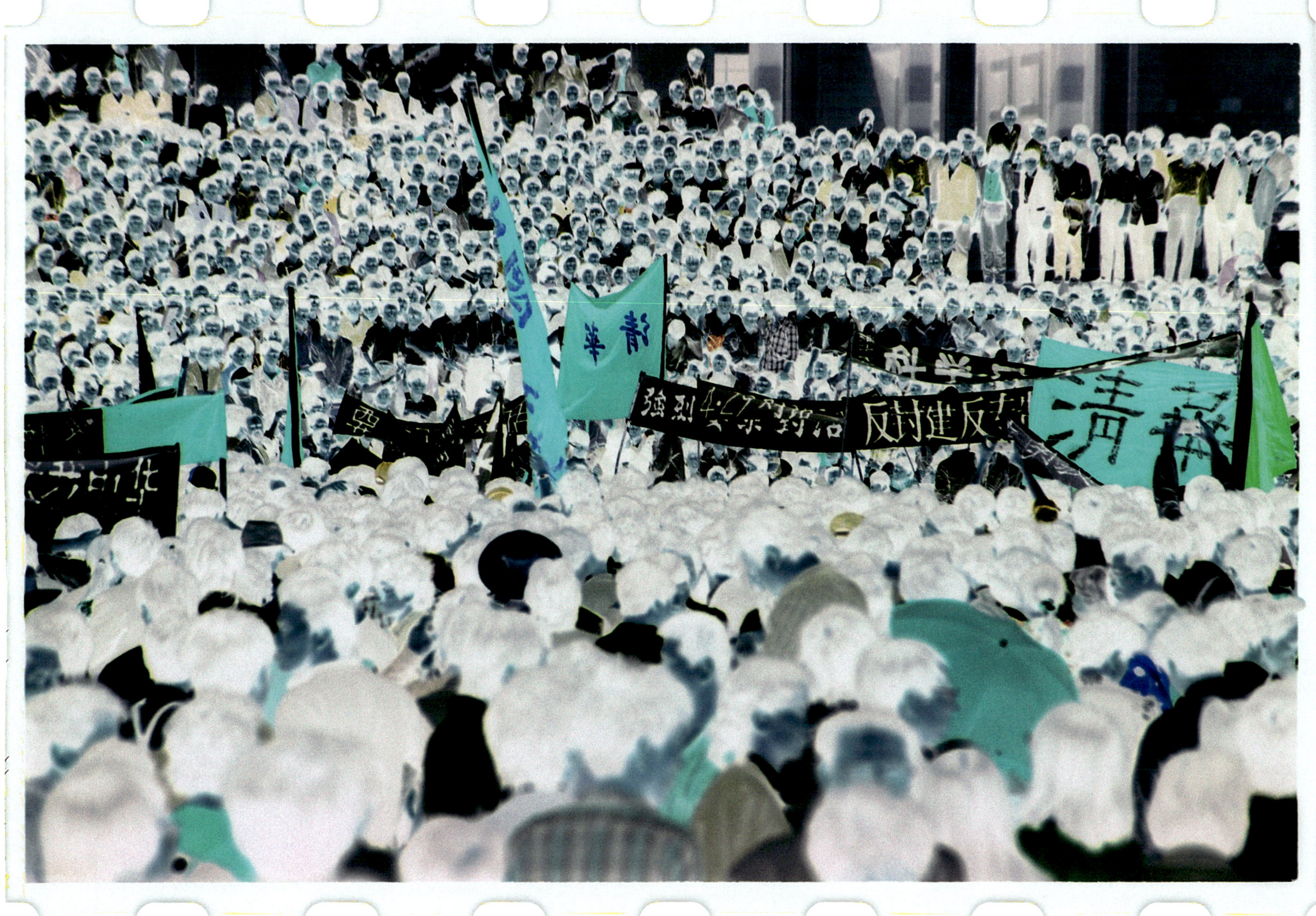

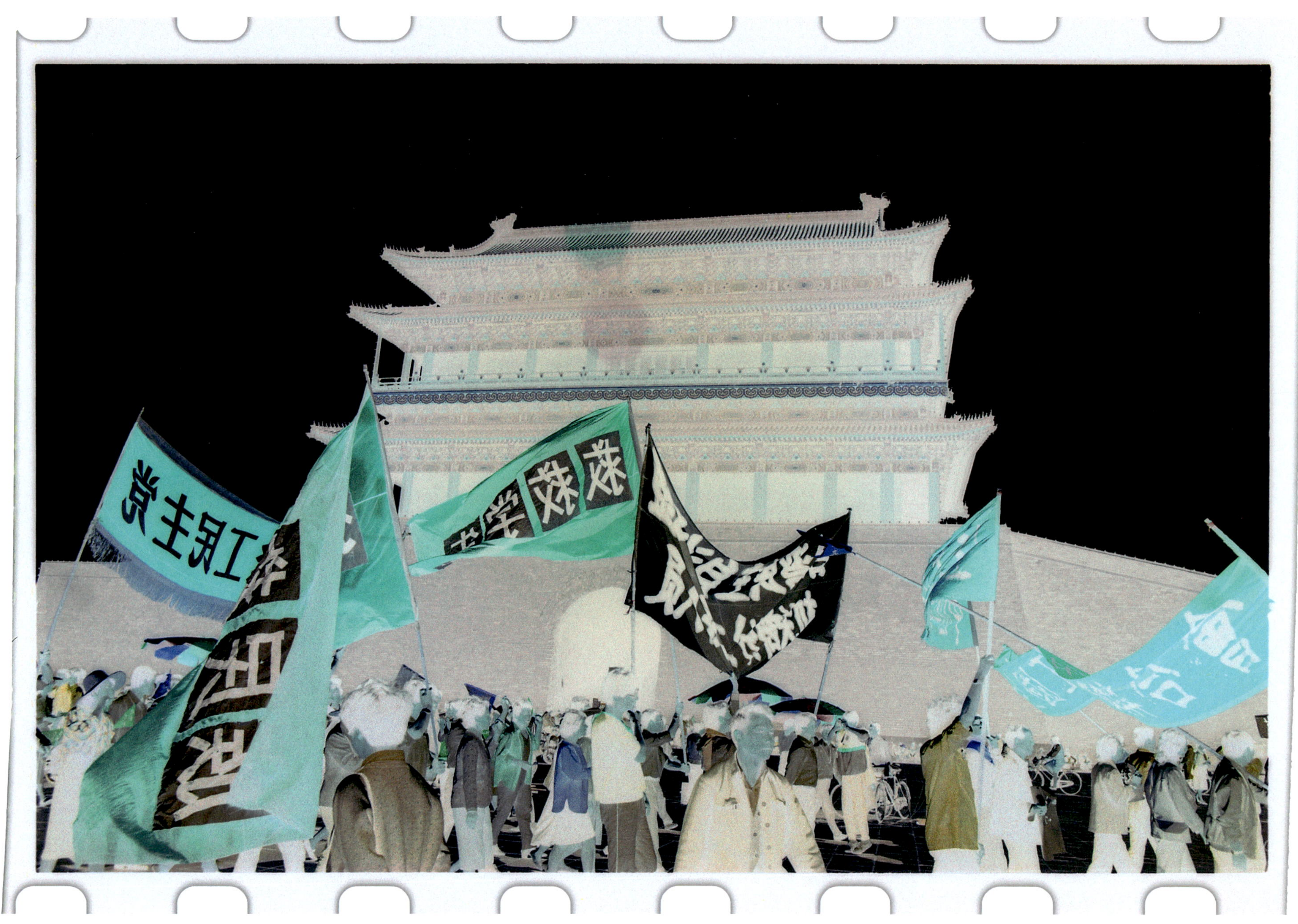

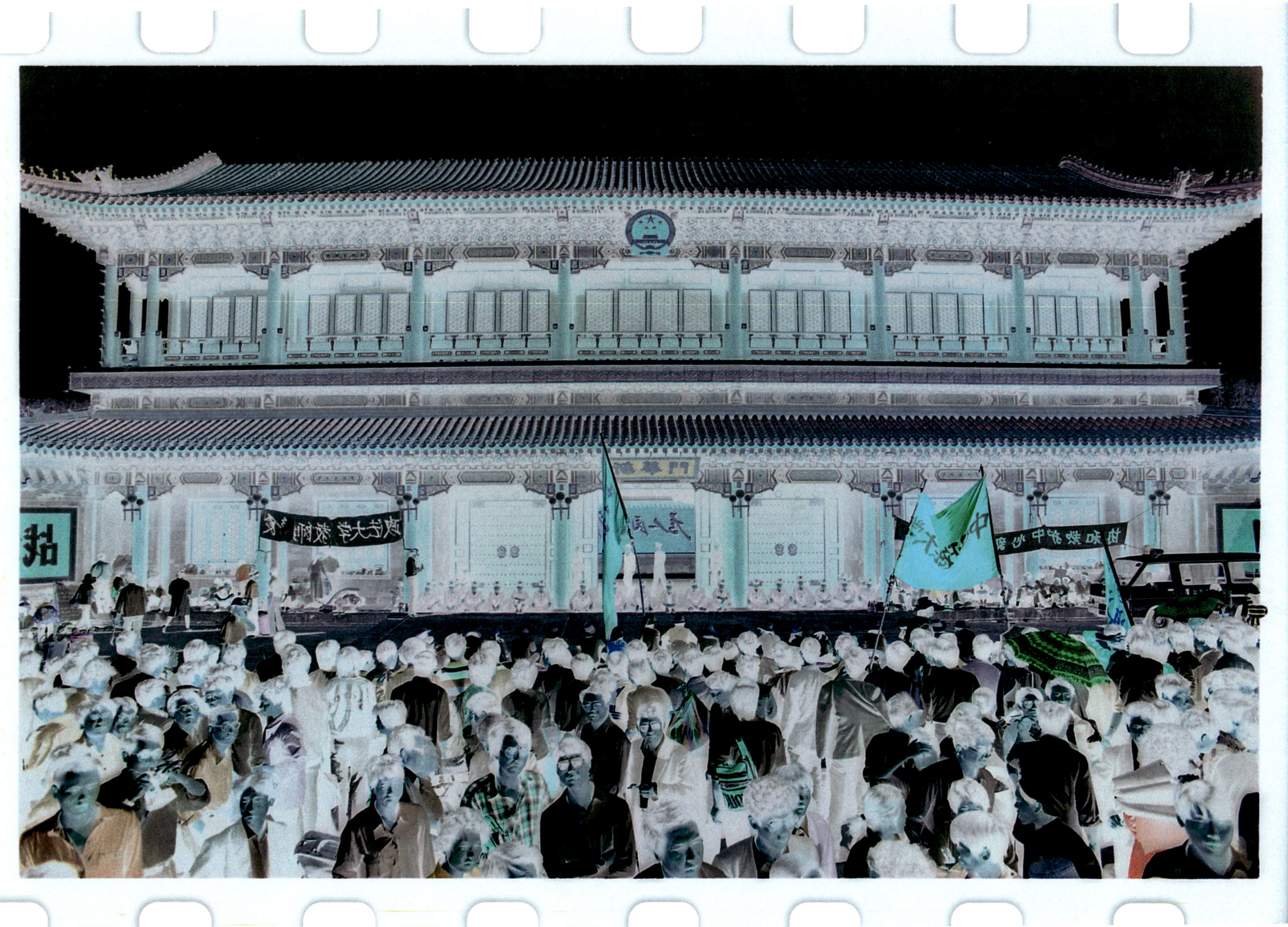

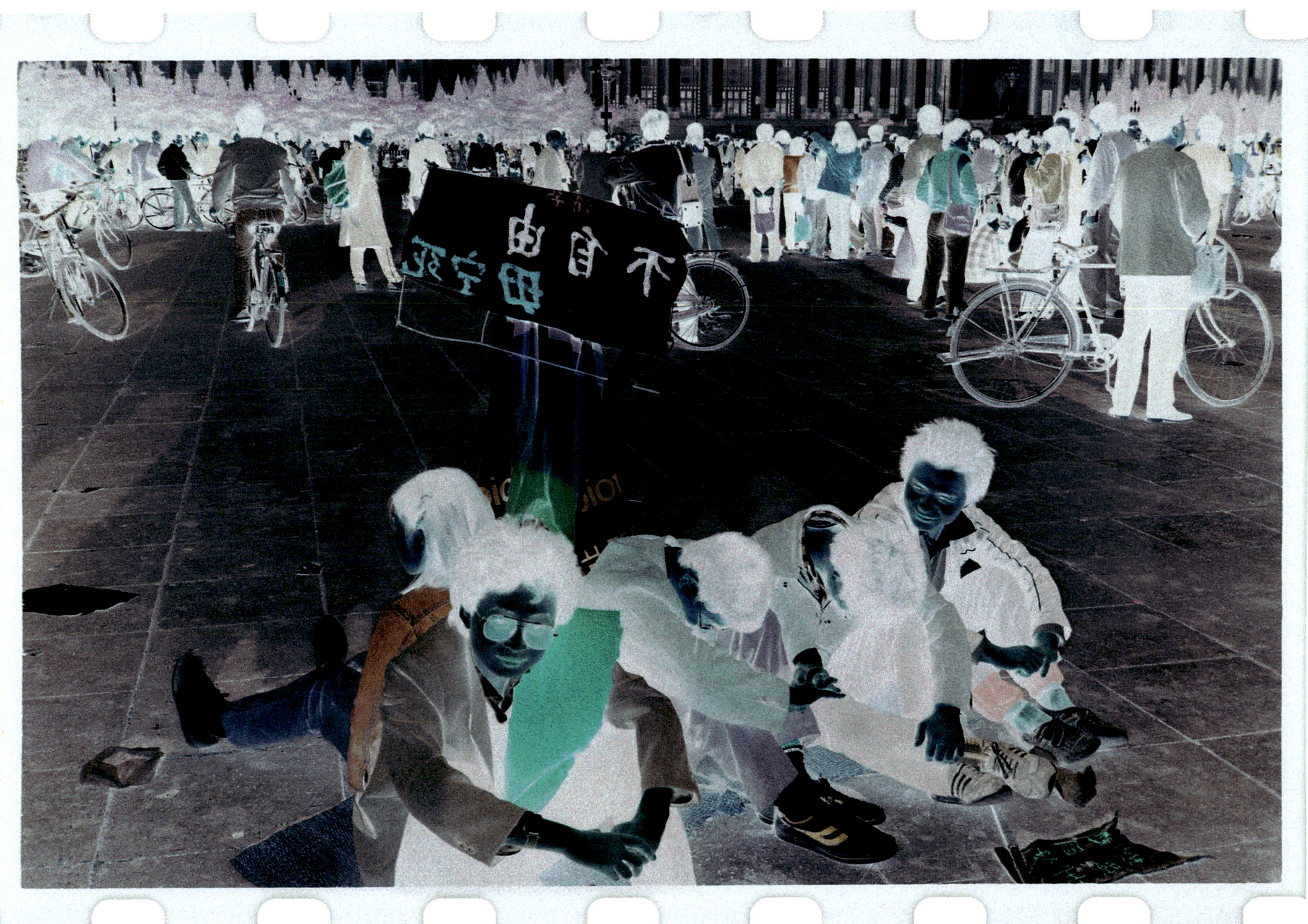

不自由毋宁死

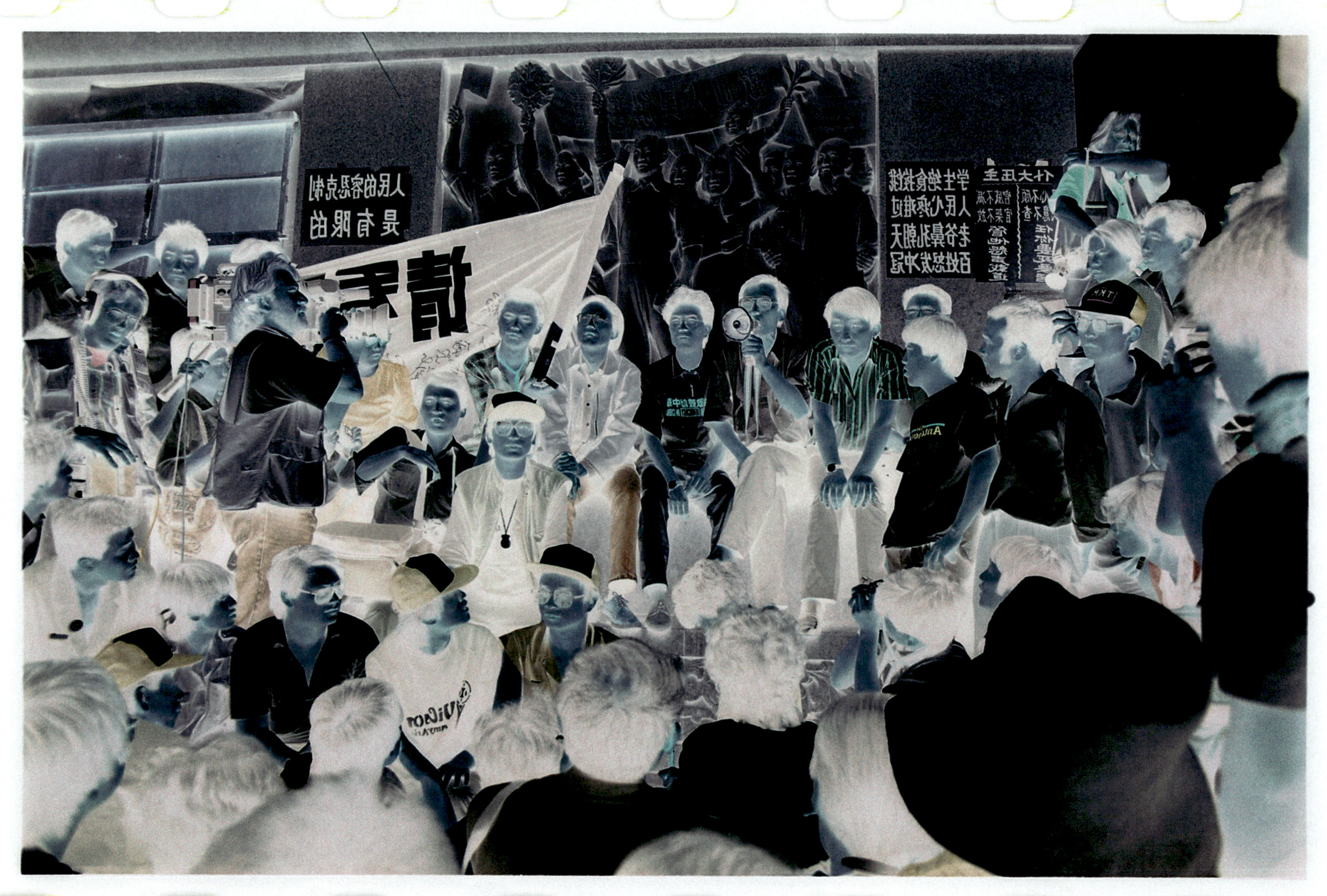

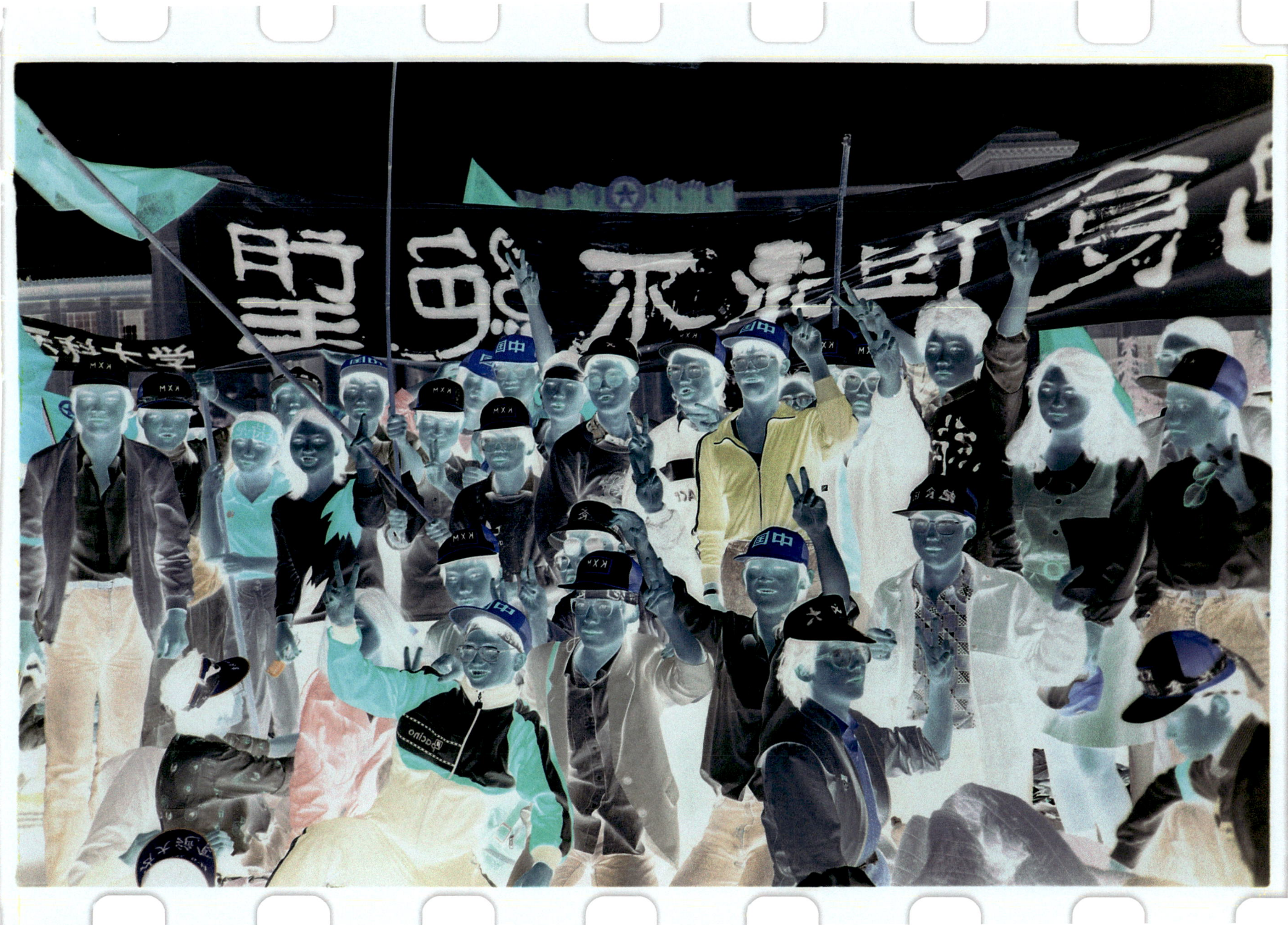

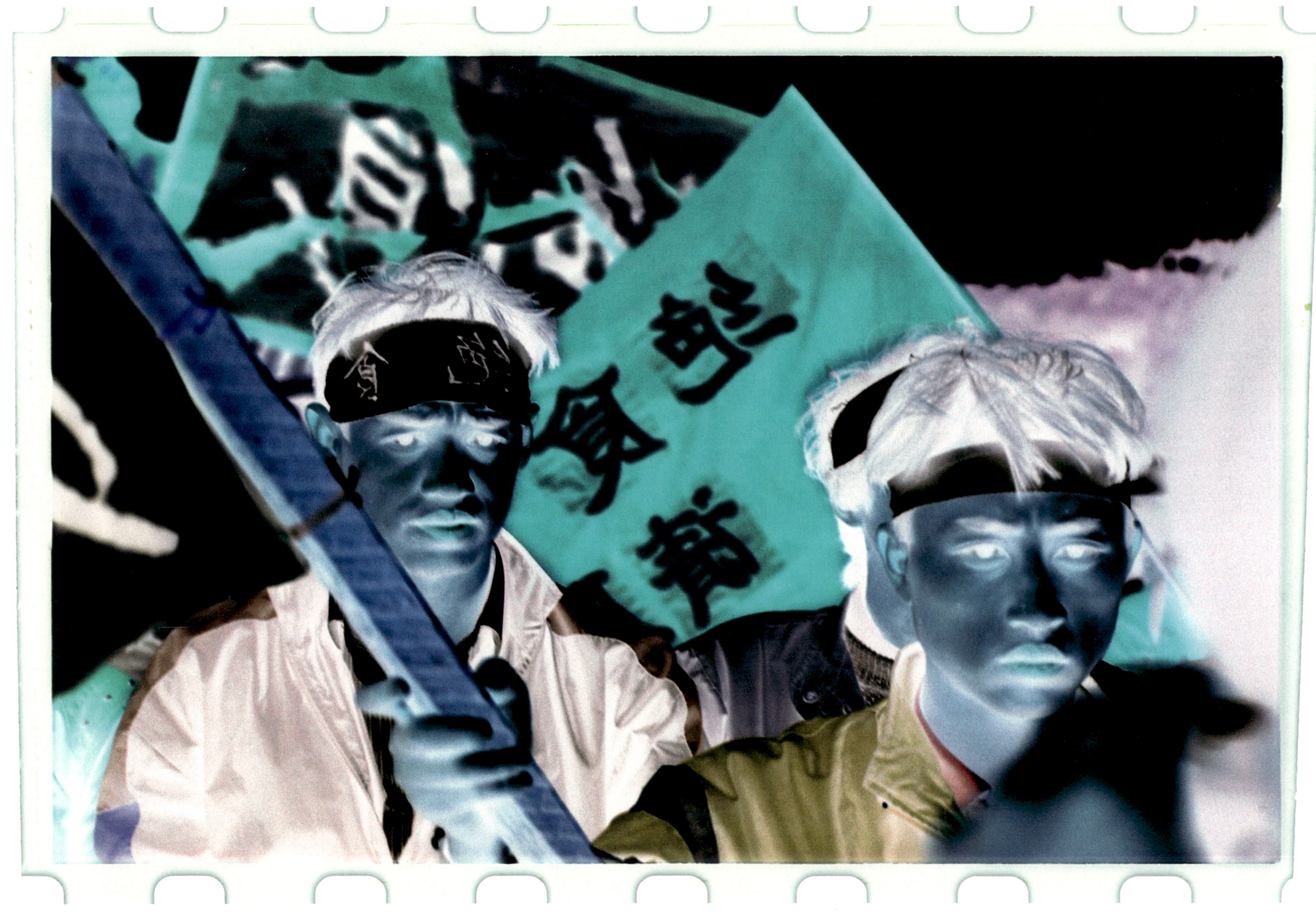

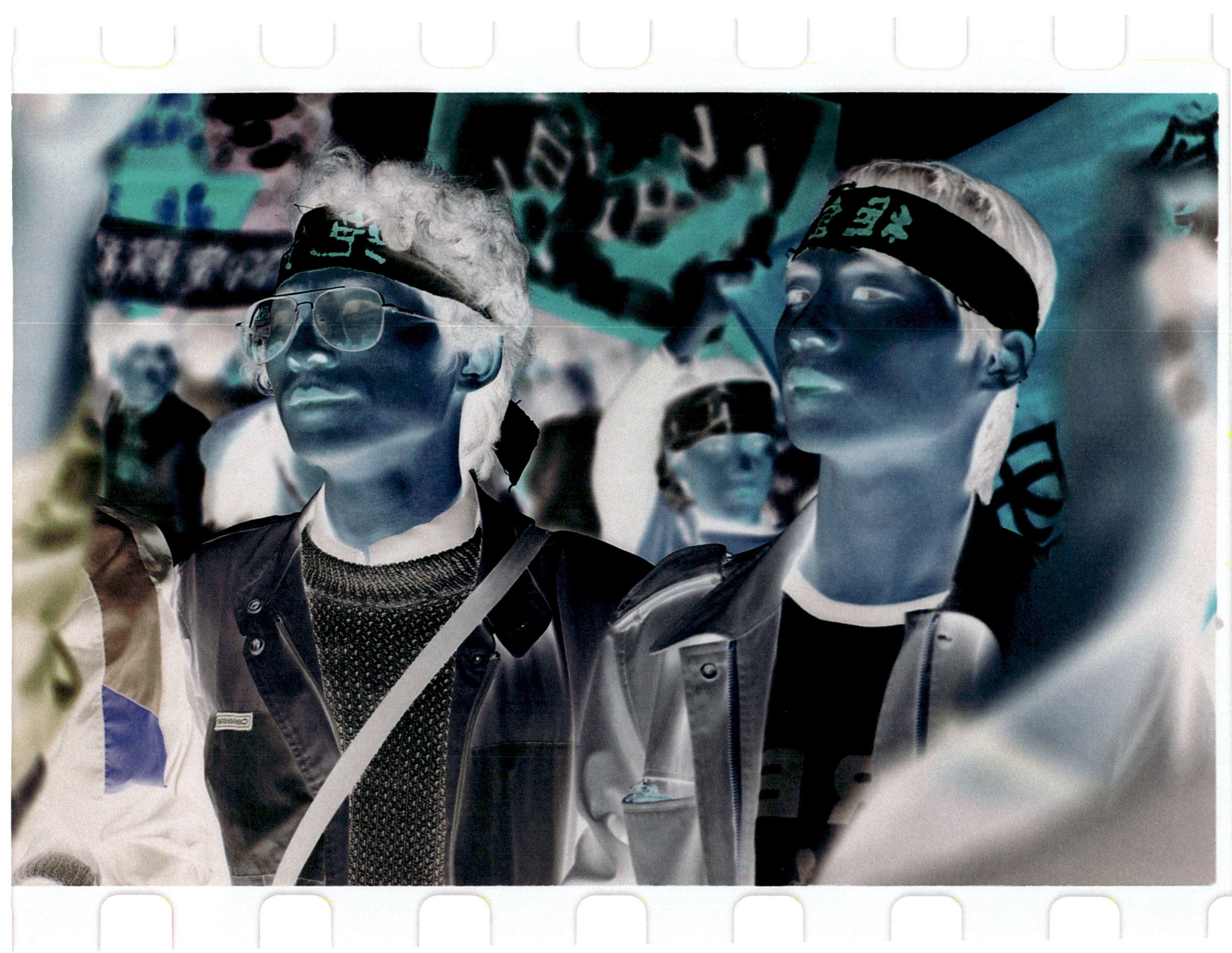

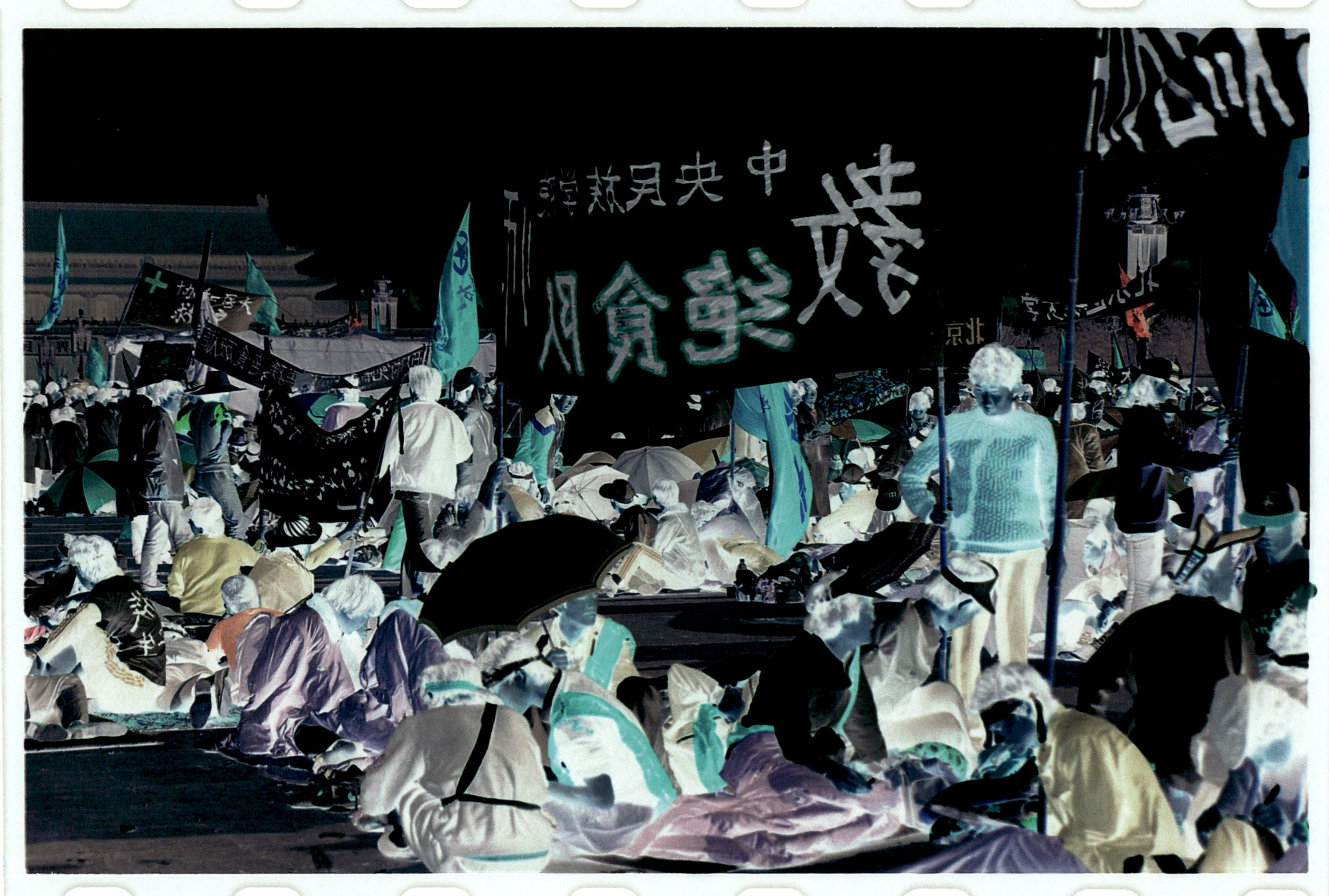

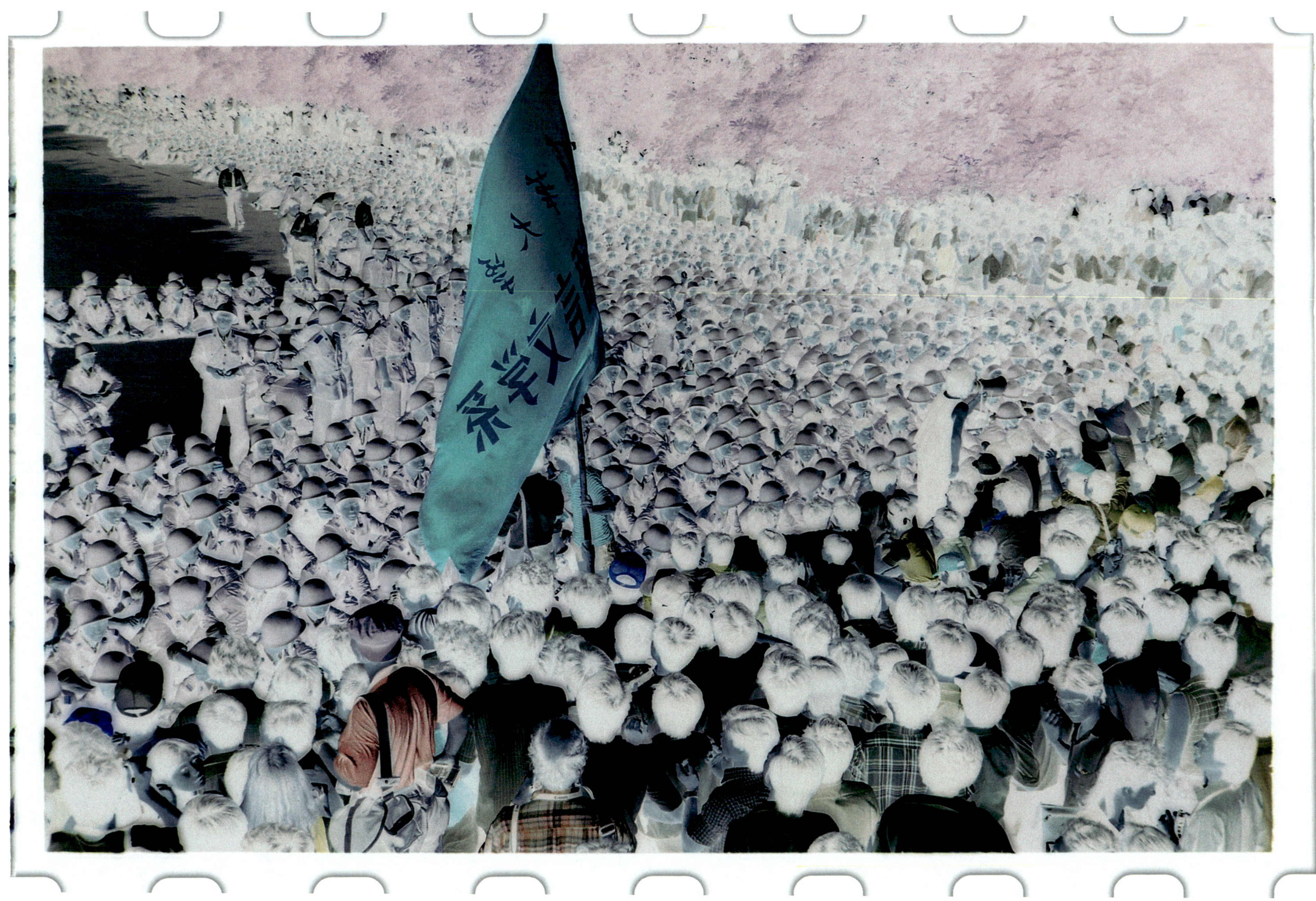

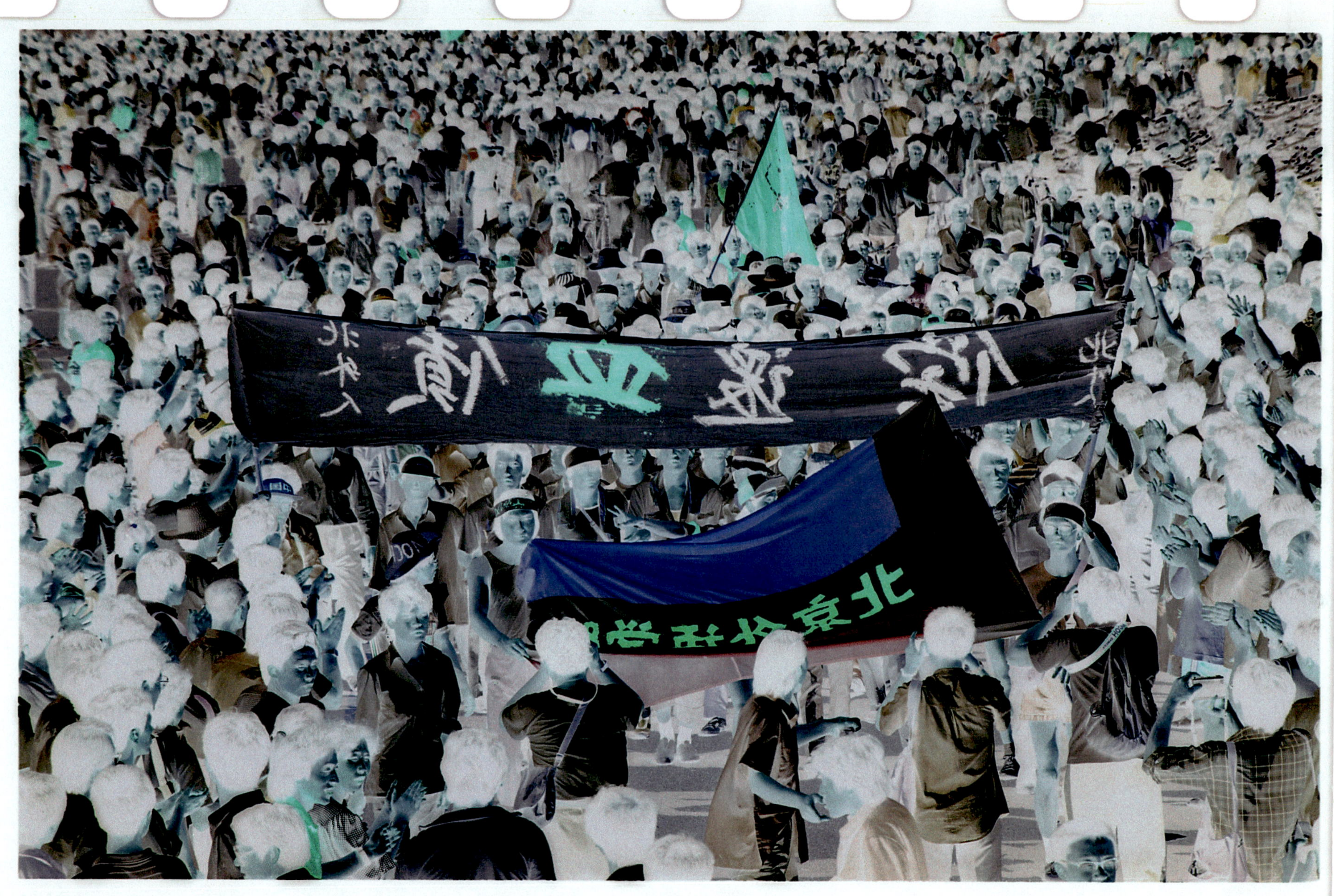

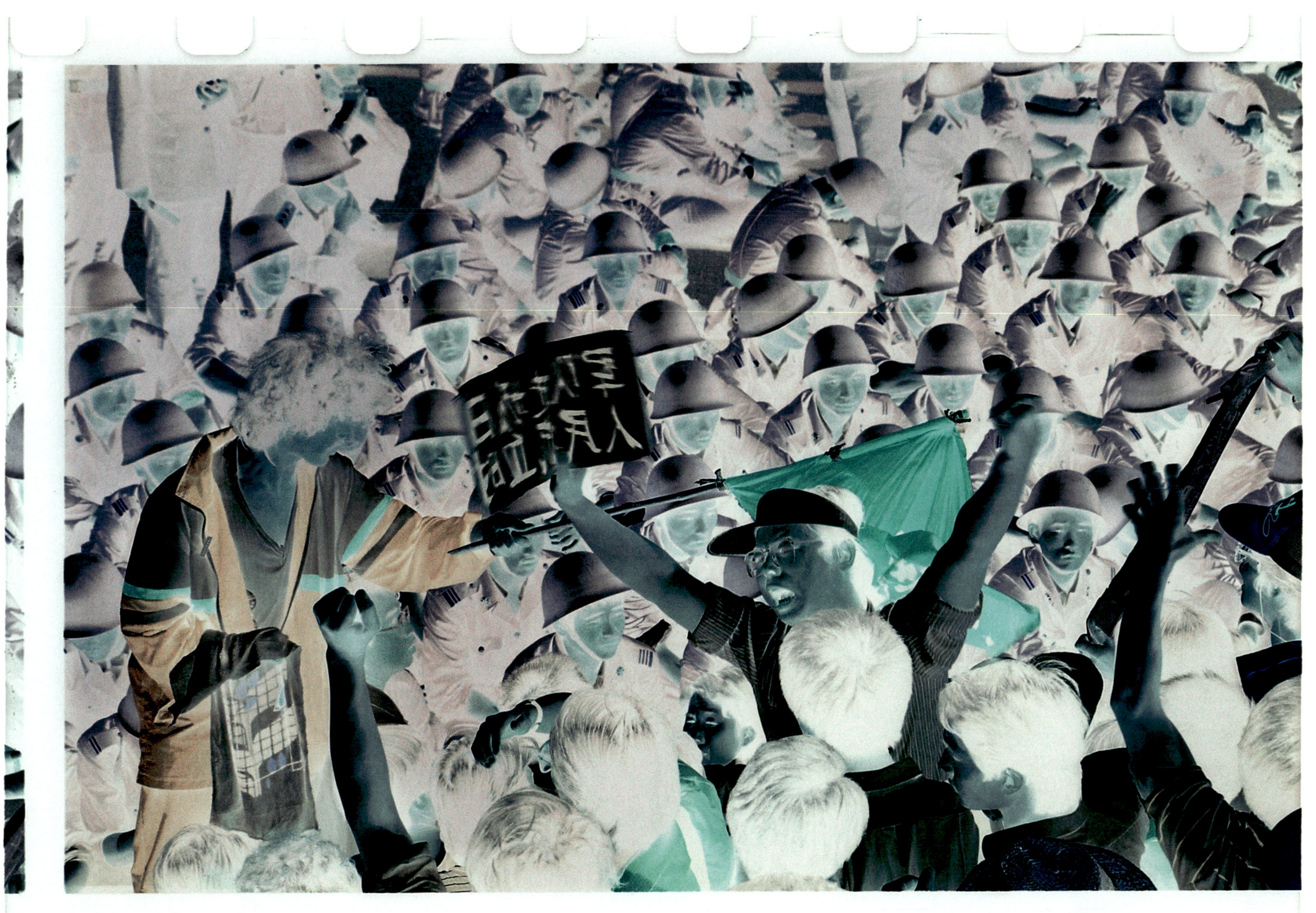

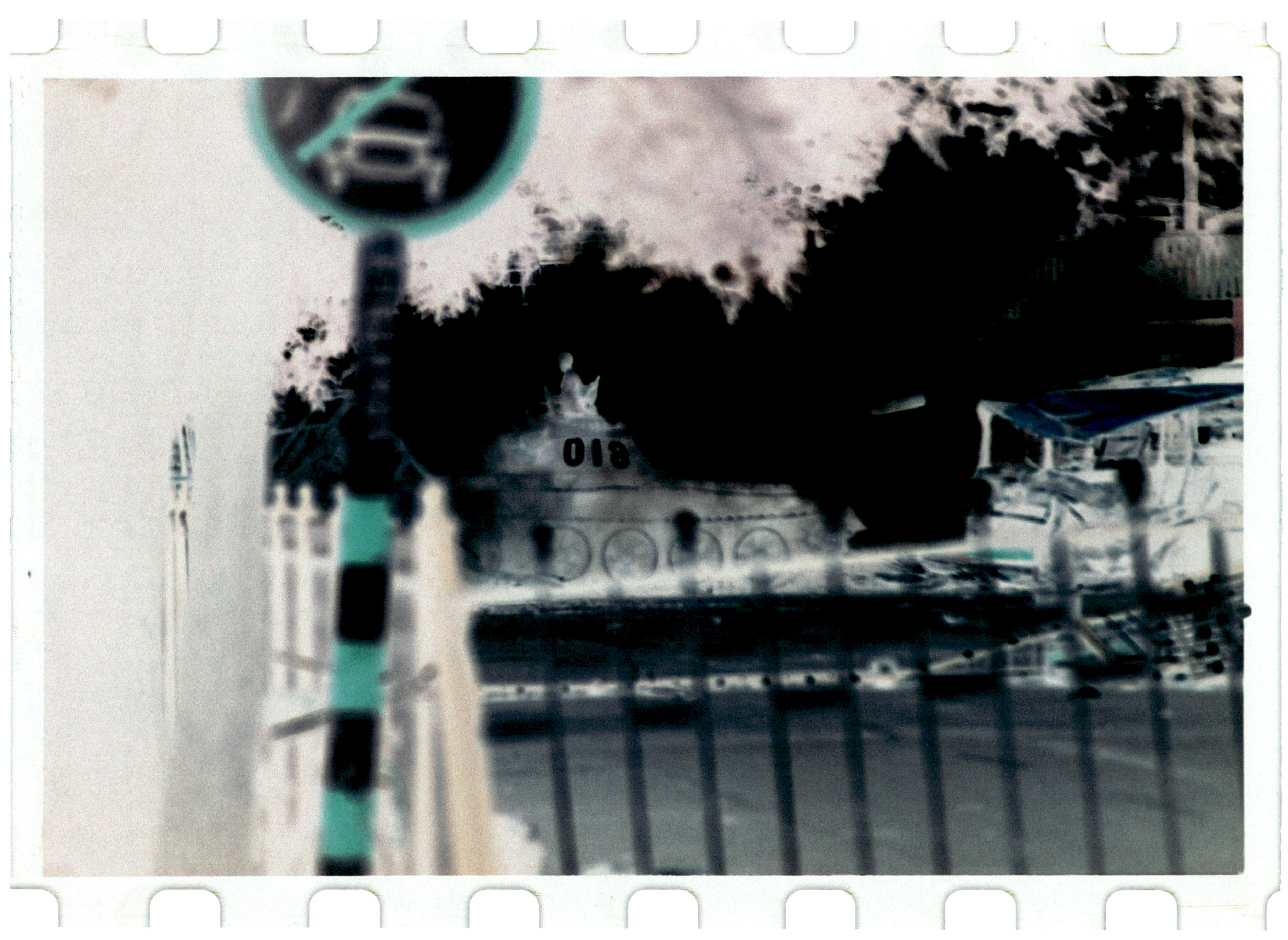

Negatives

By Shu Yang

In traditional photography, the negative image is the most direct way of capturing an analogue image through photochemistry; it is the basis of a traditional photograph. At the moment the negative image is being formed, it cannot be immediately viewed by the photographer. To really understand the photograph's entire message, the image must be completed through the powerful development process of the darkroom. Thus an important part of the traditional photographer's work is precisely anticipating the traditional negative image's visual effect. This indirect imaging skill often determined a photographer's expertise, and to other people it could feel unfamiliar and mysterious. With this indirect imaging skill, the traditional photographer takes mastery over problems, and at the same time acquires a kind of professionalism and authority that gave traditional photography a monopoly over the world of visual imagery. Before the invention of photography, this monopoly was controlled by painting, and today, this monopoly has once again been broken and seized from traditional photography by digital technology. Digital photography, through the direct use of the camera lens, obtains the image in complete accordance with the real visual image, and does not need to go through any kind of negative of the filming scene to obtain its image. The traditional photographer has lost his monopolistic authority over visual authenticity, and through the supplanting of analogue technology by digital technology, everyone can effortlessly capture the external world's true image.

Photographers are capable of examining the quality of a traditional photograph, and at the same time using the negative image to see the real world's image. Traditional photography's truthfulness was first established on the negative. As direct evidence of the real world's image, the negative was even more real than the reproduced photographs that came from it. To ordinary viewers, the photographic plate's negative image is the complete antithesis of the real world's visual authenticity. Thus, traditional photography's authenticity relies upon photographic experience in order to be constructed, and does not genuinely exist in the image itself. Photography's original purpose to both preserve the real world's living image and to create seems today, by the very nature of the media itself, to pose a challenge to objectivity. As proof of the world, traditional photography can only obtain a kind of suggestion, which is not self-evident. This characteristic of photography has been even more thoroughly interpreted by digital imagery. The visual reality of digital imagery makes it so anyone can effortlessly capture a scene and effortlessly select and falsify. Digital technology has strengthened the fictitious aspect of photography's authenticity. Digital technology has added more thoroughly to photographic transformation so that it has become possible to arbitrarily write and transform visual versions, to make it possible to satisfy even more fully the desire for a world of pictorial brilliance.

Today, in the environment of digital technology, the decline of the traditional photographic plate negative's capacity to function as the expression of truthful imagery is much like the yellowed book-binding threads of old historical books, its function as visual evidence stronger even than the words of recorded history themselves. After a quarter of a century, Xu Yong digitally scanned his negatives, shot in 1989 of the June Fourth Tiananmen incident, and presents them directly here as negative images. The purpose is to revisit this important historic event and to reflect on its continued impact. As he expressed himself: "On the attempt to cover-up and induce amnesia on an historic event, negatives have more direct impact as evidence than normal photographs or digital media. However, perhaps using this form to immunize against amnesia is not that important. What should be carefully considered are the social conditions that have resulted in the prolonged process of completing these works." Xu Yong borrows the negative image photographic plates to remind us that the Tiananmen massacre is still forbidden from public discourse by the Chinese government, and the commemoration of this unbearable reality is even further proscribed. But even more than that, they raise questions about people's collective memories of the events of June 4, 1989. In the works, the real description of history seems constrained by the dark imagery of the negatives, yet it achieves unfamiliar sensations as the eyes of the spectator are continuously seeking. These images of the June Fourth incident are similar to many other photos of the same event. Although this way of using negative photographic plates presents important historical fact, to decipher them only from the viewpoint of political correctness is not enough.

As far as the transmitting of information, Xu Yong's negatives of June Fourth would be more effective as normal photographic images than as negative images. The core meaning of Xu Yong's work "Negatives" is not only to declare the value of the photographic medium as evidence. Xu Yong uses what is revealed and illuminated in "Negatives" to remove the covers hiding morality and bravery, for traditional photography to seek new value in the digital age. This new value is not merely a continuation of traditional imagery's original rationale; it also contains a unique creativity, especially in the meaning of fine art photography.

In South Korea in December 2014 at the Gimhae Arts Center's Asia Independent Art exhibition site, Xu Yong instructed those in the audience carrying iPhones or iPads to use the "color inverse function" to view the images in "Negatives". The audience thus observed positive images as the historical truth via direct participation and interaction with the art works. This interactive feature breaks the one-dimensional visual experience of the traditional photograph album. As a result, the audience experienced not only the unveiling of the Tiananmen event, but also the relationship between the film era and digital era in an intriguing way with modern technology.

On an unprecedented global scale, the traditional photographic industry has declined rapidly. Traditional photography as information technology has lost its original value and advantage. Xu Yong's "Negatives" not only makes history and justice re-appear by refusing to forget; it also contains the basic creative concept: by transforming itself as new art, traditional photography can be reborn.

1st March 2015, Beijing, Songzhuang

底　　片

文　/　舒　陽

　　傳統底片的影像，是光化學攝影術最直接獲得的模擬影像，是獲得一張傳統照片的基礎。在獲得底片的影像時，通常不能被拍攝者直接觀察到。真正要瞭解照片的完全信息，需要通過暗房沖印才能充分確定。因此傳統攝影師的重要工作經驗，就是預估底片影像的成像效果。這種間接性的影像技術常常意味著一個攝影師的技術水準，對普通人來說具有一種陌生感和神秘感。傳統攝影師由這種間接性影像技術掌握的難度，在獲得一種專業性的同時，也獲得了一種權威性，獲得了傳統攝影對世界視覺形象真實的壟斷性。這種壟斷性，在攝影發明之前是被繪畫所把持的。而今天，這種壟斷性又被數字技術所打破並從傳統攝影中攫奪。數字技術直接將通過鏡頭獲取的影像轉換成符合視覺真實的形象，不需要再通過無法在拍攝現場直觀的底片去獲得世界的影像。傳統攝影師對視覺真實性的壟斷不再，通過數字技術對模擬技術的取代而使人人可以輕鬆抓取外在世界的真實影像。

從傳統底片中，有經驗的攝影師能夠檢驗照片的質量，並同樣將負像也看做真實世界的影像。從傳遞信息真實角度看，傳統

攝影的真實性首先建立在底片上。底片負像是比照片正像更為直接的一次性的外部世界影像。但對普通人而言，至少負像完全背離了世界的視覺真實性，底片負像是世界視覺影像真實性的徹底的反面。因此可以說，傳統攝影的真實性是依托攝影實踐經驗構建的，而不在於影像本身。攝影原為保留真實世界的逼真視覺形象而發明，在今天看來，從其媒介本身已經動搖了這種客觀性。作為世界的證據，通過傳統攝影只是獲得了一種暗示，而不是自明的。攝影的這一特性，被數字影像更加充分地詮釋了。視覺真實的數字影像可輕鬆現場抓取和輕鬆選擇、篡改。數字技術強化了攝影的這種虛擬的真實性。數字技術更加徹底地將攝影轉化成為可以任意書寫的視覺文本，使它成為更加滿足人的訴求性的世界圖景。

在今天數字技術環境中，傳統底片對表達真實影像實用功能的衰退，很像發黃的線裝書所呈現的歷史文獻，作為證據的視覺感大於歷史記載本身。時隔四分之一世紀，徐勇將他 1989 年所拍攝的「六四」事件底片經數字掃瞄直接以負像形式呈現為個人新作《底片》，意在以此反思這一重大歷史事件及現狀。他在有關自

述中寫道：「對試圖遮蔽、製造人們遺忘歷史的行為，底片比照片及數字媒介更具直接強烈的證據意義。以這種方式抗拒遺忘或證明事件也許不重要，值得關注和思考的是與這件作品相關的時間和環境因素，它們是比我更重要的作品作者」。徐勇借負像底片形式，寓意「六四」事件迄今仍被中國官方禁止談論、遑論以正常照片方式公開發表的不堪現實。這些底片似乎在質詢著人們對「六四」事件的群體記憶，在其中，對歷史的真實描述彷彿被底片的暗淡影像所壓抑，反而得到一種需要在不斷辨識中強化的陌生化效果。這些關於「六四」事件的影像，是那個時代許許多多同類影像的一部分。這樣使用負像底片方式呈現重大歷史事實，僅用政治正確性來解讀是不充分的。《底片》的核心意義，不再僅僅昭示攝影的證據價值。

如果在信息傳播的層面，徐勇應將「六四」事件的底片製成正常照片才更加有效，而不是以負像方式直接呈現。徐勇用《底片》觀照的不僅僅是影像的證據性及其去蔽的道德勇氣，還在於要為傳統攝影尋找其在數字時代新的價值系統。這個新的價值系統不但延續傳統影像的原有合理性，又具有獨特的創意性，特別是在攝影的藝術創新層面。

2014年12月，在韓國金海藝術中心舉辦的「亞洲獨立藝術連線」Asia Independent Art展覽現場，徐勇請觀眾用隨身攜帶的iPhone或iPad設置中的顏色反轉功能，在現場將作品《底片》的負像轉換成為正像來觀看，以觀眾直接參與方式揭秘作品中的歷史正像與真相。這種互動性突破了以往攝影作品或畫冊單向度的視覺經驗，不但讓觀眾參與作品所試圖體現的對天安門事件去除遮蔽的過程，更通過最新的科技成果將攝影的膠片時代與數字時代的關係巧妙而富有趣味地加以呈現。

規模空前的全球性傳統膠片工業在幾年間迅速衰亡，意味著作為信息技術的傳統攝影失去原有價值優勢。徐勇的《底片》，除了再次使歷史與正義以新的面目拒絕被遺忘，它所蘊含的基本創作觀念在於：成為新的藝術，傳統攝影可以重獲新生。

2015年3月1日，北京宋莊

Xu Yong

Fine art photographer, born in Shanghai in 1954, resident of Beijing.

Major publications of serial photographic works:

Hutong 101 Photos, 1989

Opening Beijing, 2001

Xiaofangjia Hutong, 2003

Backdrops and Backdrops, 2006

Solution Scheme, 2007

18% Gray, 2010

This Face, 2011

徐 勇

攝影藝術家．1954 年生於上海．居住北京。

代表作品：

《胡同 101 像》．1989 年

《開放北京》．2001 年

《小方家胡同》．2002 年

《佈景與背景》．2006 年

《解決方案》．2007 年

《十八度灰》．2010 年

《這張臉》．2011 年

Through the Looking Glass

Gérard A. Goodrow

What is *reality?* Philosophers have been debating this question for centuries. At the very latest since the Age of Enlightenment, it has become clear that reality is based more than anything else on experience and the rational analysis of this, rather than on dogma promulgated by authority. And since experience is first and foremost individual, reality is necessarily subjective. Despite numerous attempts by those in power to dictate reality in the form of official historiography, the personal experiences of the people continually take hold as a form of collective memory, which inevitably leads to the emergence of a "reality" that often has little or nothing to do with that propagated by the state.

What actually happened on Tiananmen Square on June 4, 1989? Official coverage of the "incident" on the part of the Chinese authorities varies greatly from the viewpoints taken by Western journalists. The many verbal, written, and photographic/filmed reports by eyewitnesses present at Tiananmen Square that fateful day also vary enormously, so that it is nearly impossible to get a clear picture of what actually took place, let alone why. Xu Yong was on site at the very epicentre of the tumultuous events that occurred that day in the heart of Beijing. Armed with his camera, Xu shot dozens of images of those present – snapshots taken quickly and seemingly at random in what appears to be an attempt to capture the volatile atmosphere of the situation rather than striving to create an objective documentary reportage. These images reflect his own individual reality and thus tell his own personal side of the story unfolding before him.

More than 26 years later, we are confronted with these images, which trigger our collective memory and colour our proxy experience of the historic incident. But do Xu's images really provide us with any worthwhile information? Do they in any way contribute to the clarification of what actually took place that day? No, they do not – but that is precisely what they strive not to do. Xu Yong's images are not intended as documentation, but rather reveal how we deal with the concepts of documentation and reality, and how these are transformed into history.

The very existence of the negative means that (analogue) photographs always go through a process of transformation.

The photo is shot, the film is developed, and the image is finally printed by means of light passing through the semitransparent negative. Like the children's game of "Chinese Whispers", during which a simple statement is subtly changed as it is passed down the line, much can happen during the multistage transformation of the image of reality caught on film into an image of purported reality captured on paper. There is much talk about the authenticity of the image in the various texts on Xu Yong's Negatives, but this is actually secondary – for how do we truly know that these images have not been manipulated? It is a matter of faith. And how does one define manipulation in the first place? All photographs are subjective in the sense that the photographer consciously chooses not only his subject, but also the detail and the perspective. The photo is thus not an image of reality – even when it has not been manipulated physically (or digitally) – but rather a filtered image of reality, seen and experienced by the very human photographer at a particular moment in time.

What is more, with Xu's Negatives, the viewer is invited to actively participate, to interact with the images, albeit though yet another filter. Using the digital technology made available by smart phones and tablets, the viewer can transform the photos from negative into positive images. But is any more information made available as a result? Is one any closer to the historical event? To be honest, the images themselves are not very different from many we have already seen. But that is not the point. By presenting the inverted, negative images, he strengthens their suggestive power. I am reminded of the earliest examples of true "free art" in the west, namely Goya's depiction of the execution of Spanish rebels by Napoleon's occupational army (El tres de mayo de 1808 en Madrid, 1814) and Géricault's disquieting image of the maritime tragedy of the French frigate Méduse on July 2, 1816 (The Raft of the Medusa, 1818–19). In both cases, the paintings were created several years after the historically significant events. And in both cases, the artists manipulated history to make a specific point – in favour of the victims and against the powers that be. Nevertheless, despite various ahistorical anomalies within the paintings, the purpose of which was to influence our reception of the images and, with this of the events themselves, both images have been branded into collective memory as historically accurate documentation of the respective incident. Does Xu Yong do the same with his inverted photographic "documents"?

In the context of the artist's other photographic series, the true import of his Negatives is revealed. In Backdrops and Backdrops (2007), for example, Xu presents tourist-like "snapshots" of normal people in front of the entrance to the Forbidden City in Beijing as well as in front of the famous Oriental Pearl Tower in Shanghai – the one backdrop representing the ancient imperial history of China, as well as the appropriation of this for propaganda purposes by Chairman Mao; the other being a popular symbol of China's ultra-modern present and future as a leader within the global economy. At first glance, it is difficult to discern whether the landmarks in the backgrounds are real or merely backdrops in a photographic studio. Like his Negatives, the Backdrops are indeed "real", but does that make them any more "authentic", or do they remain at the level of "docu-fiction"? And what about his photobook Xiaofangjia Hutong, for which Xu photographed residents of a traditional hutong in Beijing in the summer of 2002? Two months later, the neighbourhood was razed, and the residents gone – all in the name of "progress"

and unfortunately not a singular event. Here as well, Xu's photos are all that remain and thus serve to feed our collective memory – albeit once again from the artist's own personal perspective.

I am reminded of Lewis Carroll's groundbreaking novel Through the Looking Glass (1871). Here as well, the concept of reality is called into question. The world on the other side of the mirror is, at first glance, topsy-turvy and at times even frightening. With time, however, Alice discovers the logic of this strange, superficially nonsensical realm. At the end of the story, Alice awakens from her "dream" and recalls the speculation of the strange Tweedle brothers that everything might in fact be a dream dreamt by the Red King, meaning that Alice herself would actually be no more than a mere figment of the king's imagination.

What is real? What can we believe? Are our actions truly our own, or are we "guided" by powers unbeknownst to us? By inverting the ostensibly objective world, Xu Yong provides us with the key to enter the realm "beyond the looking glass". What we then make of this situation is up to us and us alone …

Epilogue

Martin Rendel

Why republish a book that has already been banned?

I was born in a democratic country in the late 1960s. While my grandparents experienced war under a totalitarian regime and my parents were raised in the period of reconstruction that followed, my own generation, as well as the generations since, did not have to struggle – neither for peace, nor for prosperity. Stable political and economic conditions are something we take for granted in Western Europe - a very comfortable situation, I must admit. Although we are aware of opposite situations in other parts of the world, we regard them from a great distance and with a sense of apathy.

Then came 1989 – a year significantly marked by political upheavals in the European Eastern Bloc countries, which were brought about by growing protest among the people. Following the dismantling of the border between Hungary and Austria in May, the first democratic parliamentary elections in Poland in June, the fall of the Berlin Wall in November, and the elimination of border fortifications between Czechoslovakia and Germany in December, the Iron Curtain was finally opened. This initiated the end of the Cold War and marked the conclusion of the 'short 20th century', making 1989 one of the most important years in the long history of democracy.

Also in the People's Republic of China, the hope for more freedom of speech and participation of the people flared up for a few weeks. As in Germany, it began slowly, by the gathering of average people in public places. But the outcome was quite different... Whatever happened on Tiananmen Square in that summer of 1989, it has left China with a trauma.

When we talk about 1989 in Germany, most people revel in cheerful memories and try to remember where they were the day the Berlin Wall came down. When you mention 1989 in a conversation in China, people become silent. For the younger generation, it is something they usually do not know much about. The older generations have learned that the 'Tiananmen incident' is something one does not talk about – at least not openly. What is more, reliable sources of information about the incident are difficult to find, as though it were to be erased from history.

Xu Yong was there – a young man in his mid-thirties, armed with his camera – from the peaceful beginning in late April to the abrupt and brutal end on the 4th of June.

When I saw his pictures for the first time, they touched me in a profound way, even though they have neither subtitles nor comments. It is even difficult to see anything at all, unless you know how to invert the colours with a smartphone. They depict neither drama nor brutality. They do not blame or judge. But they do document – with a certain discreteness of presentation and with something very simple and yet enormously powerful: hope.

Xu Yong is a chronicler of that hope. His book makes a particular moment of history tangible. And I finally came to understand that democracy – whether it is an ideal form of government or not – is a decision. Not of a ruling minority, but of the people. It is built upon the constant political commitment of the people, also my own.
Thank you, Xu Yong, for this lesson.

This is, in my opinion, why this book should be republished.

Title: Negatives
Author: Xu Yong
Texts: Shu Yang, Gérard Goodrow, Martin Rendel
Editors: Martin Rendel & Cathrine Cheng / K26 Sino-German Art Association, Beijing
                Markus Schaden / ThePhotoBookMuseum, Cologne
                Richard Reisen / Verlag Kettler, Dortmund

K26

The PhotoBookMuseum

Design: Liu Song
                Frederic Lezmi (Cover)
                Richard Reisen
Published by: Verlag Kettler, Dortmund
                www.verlag-kettler.de
Production: Druckerei Kettler, Bönen
                www.druckerei-kettler.de

ISBN: 978-3-86206-529-5